—I found this book to be a real treasure. With clarity, humor and loving detachment, Amma gently pulls aside the veil to illuminate the true nature of what it means to be a spiritual being having a human experience. The book interweaves profound insights with a collection of processes for increasing consciousness, breaking old patterns and claiming power over your experience as a human being. Amma offers an abundance of concepts and tools; you can freely pick and choose those that are relevant and supportive now, and return to see what inspires you at a later time. I found the concepts and insights to be deeply supportive of my own spiritual journey, and have made effective use of many of the processes. I am grateful to Amma, and to Cathy as her channel, for the gifts that are so generously offered here.

—Shaina Noll

The *Heart* *Doorway* to *Your* *Power*

Amma Through Cathy Chapman

Cathy Chapman, PhD

Leah-el Publishing
Houston, Texas
2012

Leah-el Publishing
7800 Amelia Rd. Suite 10
Houston, TX 77055
Email leahelpublishing@gmail.com
Fax 832-615-3050

13 Digit ISBN Number: 978-1-937474-00-3
10 Digit ISBN Number: 1-937474-00-3

www.AmmaTheDivineMother.com
www.SpiritualLoveFare.com
www.OdysseyToWholeness.com

Publishing Consultant & Book Project Coordinator — Rita Mills
Editor — Donna M. Griffith
Cover Design — John D. Long, III
Text Design — Rita Mills

The information in this book is just that, information. It is to inform, educate and entertain only. In no way is anything in this book designed to diagnose, treat, heal or prevent any dis-ease or disorder you may have. Any health concerns, be they physical or emotional, should be taken to your health care provider. You are responsible for how you use the material in the following pages. In fact, you are responsible for all your thoughts, words and actions. Remember, that the allopathic community prefers you do what they say in regards to their preferred methods of surgery and various chemicals and radiation. Except for a small percentage of practitioners, they are not interested in you taking responsibility for your own well-being. You have access to your deep inner knowing. Tap into it and use it, not only for your personal health care, but also in reading this or any other material.

Dedication

This book is dedicated to all who have played their roles so well in my life. From you I have remembered what love is...and what love isn't. I have learned how I can be healer to others...and how I can wound. I have learned of the complexities of attempting to find my way in this grand world of ours.

I especially dedicate this book to the aspect of God who has chosen to come through me in such a powerful way. Amma the Divine Mother, I know you are my mother and that I grew in your womb before I began the sojourn of my Soul. I thank you for allowing me to bring in some small part of your loving energy and share yours with others.

From the religion of my childhood, I learned I was made in the image and likeness of God and that God is Love. Through you, I have learned I Am Love Incarnate. Through you, I have learned everyone is Love Incarnate.

Through you, I have learned the only action you are capable of doing is loving...and how grand and awe-some is your Love. Thank you.

Acknowledgements

I'd like you to know how many people it takes to bring a project such as this to fruition. To understand how important these people have been to me, it is crucial you know something about me. Ideas are never a problem for me. I have so many ideas they overwhelm me, as well as others. Ahh, but the ability to manage the details to put these ideas into action…perhaps you can find them in the little toenail of my right foot. I often can't find that skill at all. This is why the following people have been so important to me.

My words for this book came through a series of messages from the being I know as Amma the Divine Mother. She is the feminine aspect of God. I was raised with God the Father. Amma is God the Mother. These are her words translated from the energy coming through me. Any mistakes in translation are solely mine.

The problem that presented itself to me was how to get these messages off the recorder and then edited. I could handle getting them off the recorder, but transcribing them was another issue. This is where my dear friend Donna Griffith came in. She has done the transcribing for me since the beginning and I trust will continue for many years. She is truly "the wind beneath my wings."

Donna also has a clear connection with Amma. When she transcribes she communicates with Amma about how to edit the material. The spoken word and written word are different. Donna works to make things grammatical and easy to read. She has told me there are times she will begin to reword something and receives the clear message, "No, that's how I want it."

After Donna's initial editing, each message was sent to the *Sedona Journal of Emergence* where they were first published. Thank you Melody O'Ryin Swanson for first letting me know these messages from Amma the Divine Mother were for the world.

What is written always needs to be edited several times for spelling, spacing, grammar and clarity. Angel Sandoval and Irene Boudle have been wonderful supports. (Any errors you find are my responsibility as I didn't always follow what Angel and Irene suggested.) I thank you for your willing and loving service. You have made this a better book.

All these words need to be placed upon the page in a pleasing manner. If you're like me, you just thought it happened magically. It doesn't. This is where my friend, Rita Mills, comes in. Thank you so much for your diligent and wonderful formatting.

Thank you, John Long, for the wonderful book cover. You are a gifted designer and I take delight in how well we work together. Check out his web site at sohryn.net.

Many thanks to Howard Batie. He gave me permission to use his wife's diagram of the chakras. You can find them in his book *Healing Body, Mind & Spirit: A Guide to Energy-Based Healing.* All you energy healers may want to check it out. It's in its fifth printing with Llewellyn Publications.

The wonderful forward is by Robert Pettit, PhD. He is an amazing man and wonderful healer. Dr. Pettit is a retired emeritus professor from Texas A&M University and the author of two newly published spiritually centered books. These books have been dictated by Spirit and are designed to help anyone interested in ascending to the "New Earth." They are entitled "Physical Body Ascension to The New Earth—Instruction Manual" and "Wake Up For Ascension To a New Earth—or Leave."

As any family member or friend of a writer knows, people, and in this case pets, can be neglected during the writing process. So, thank you Frick and Frack for pestering me to pay attention to you, and chewing on the legs of the chair so I absolutely have to take you for a walk. I expect to have you both many years to perform this service for me…and we'll play fetch more often.

You, dear readers, are so very important. These messages are for you. As you use the information contained within, you assist in raising the vibration of the planet. We all join together to bring healing to this world during the dawning of this wondrous New Age.

Table of Contents

Introduction

Power is a tricky subject.

Two statements about power come to mind. "Power corrupts and absolute power corrupts absolutely" was stated in 1887 by Baron John Emerich Edward Dalberg Acton. The Twentieth Century comment is one of the Twelve Steps of Alcoholics Anonymous: "We admitted we were powerless over alcohol and our lives had become unmanageable." In both cases there is an implication that power is negative.

Most people view power as being "over" someone . . . your parents, boss, the police, the government and teachers. Even friends or spouses have power "over". Power is equated with being able to force someone to do something the other doesn't want. Does paying taxes come to mind?

In this book, power is discussed as an integral aspect of life. This is personal power. Most people do not realize they have power and few know how to access it. Unfortunately, power "over" someone is what we see most commonly in the news, at work and in other areas of our lives. This is the lower vibrational use of power. True power, the power that comes from within, is rare.

True power is accessed through knowledge and discipline. Few people know they can learn to activate the power inherent within them. This power is found through the right use of the mind, consciousness and the human energy field. Power is accessed by using the one and only substance from which we were all made…Love.

What love is has been distorted beyond recognition. People don't recognize Love is the Power. Each person was created from Love. Love is the Source of Creation and is the Creator Itself, no matter what name you apply to Source. We can learn to share in this creative power. Unfortunately, few people have been raised with this knowledge. *The Heart: Doorway to Power* introduces you to the means hidden within you to activate your innate power.

Inspiration

Inspiration for any project comes from somewhere. Even when that inspiration comes from deep within, it comes from a place beyond the human persona. Some call this place God, Universal Consciousness, Love, Buddha, Krishna, Allah or another name. My inspiration goes by the name of Amma the Divine Mother.

If you're not familiar with her body of work published in the *Sedona Journal of Emergence*, let me tell you a little about her and how she became my inspiration.

My mom introduced me to mysticism through the Catholic Charismatic Renewal in 1970. I was active in this movement for more than ten years. There I became aware of the Gifts of the Spirit, the more fascinating of which for on-lookers was praying in tongues. The only time I could consistently sing on key was when I was singing in tongues. In addition, I learned about the gift of prophecy which is receiving a message from God or "a word from the Lord." There are other gifts, two of which are leadership and healing.... "And the greatest of these is Love."

In December of 1975, my spiritual journey brought me to join a wonderful group of women in a community known as the Dominican Sisters of Houston, Texas. I lived, prayed, served and learned with them for the next twenty years. In February of 1996, I pulled away from this community as I delved more deeply into mysticism and discovered energy based healing through a program known as Healing Touch. My concept of God began to evolve and could no longer be held in the confines of the Roman Catholic Church or Christianity.

In 2002 an energy—a being—began to fill me, wanting me to express the energy in words. I had felt that same energy while in the Charismatic Renewal. I knew it was God bringing a message. When I asked, "Who are you?" she responded, "I Am Amma the Divine Mother of the divine mothers and I am your mother."

What I called the gift of prophecy in the Catholic Charismatic Renewal, is called channeling in the spirituality I was now experiencing. Channeling is opening oneself to the Love of God and allowing that message to come through you. Anyone can channel just as anyone can receive a message from Spirit. Anyone, that means you the reader, can be inspired by God.

As you will discover in Chapter 1, this book began with me sitting down at my computer asking Amma questions about power. Over the next months, she gave me perspectives on power in various situations. Most, if not all of these messages, were published individually in *The Sedona Journal of Emergence*.

As you read these messages, do so from your heart. You do this by moving your awareness from your head to your heart. How? Think of someone you care for deeply. Feel the love you have for that person or a beloved pet. Notice where you experience these feelings. This is the heart emotional center. When you read this book, have your awareness in this area of your body.

Have a notebook with you as you read. Record your reflections, your inspirations. Listen with your heart. It is through your heart you will find your power.

Enjoy. Expand. Be in peace.

Foreword

Your guidance system led you to pick up this book. This is an indication your spiritual helpers considered the information within "it" has value for improving your health and well-being. As you read the information within this book, supplied through Cathy Chapman from the female aspect of God called Amma, you will discover some very important procedures for taking your power back. To take your power back involves gaining an understanding there is nothing outside of you that has power over you. You will discover that the internal wake-up guiding you from within has guided you to seek out spiritual help outlined within this book, *The Heart: Doorway to Your Power*. The information presented can help you prepare for and adjust to these rapidly changing times.

Throughout this book, you will be guided to free yourself from external and internal thought-forms (beliefs and programs) that have limited your capability to know you are an unlimited creation. You will come to understand and know you have the power within yourself to create the life you have always dreamed about.

You can discover that your choice to come to Earth this incarnation had a definite purpose. That choice and purpose involved the desire to experience separation and participate in a series of meaningful experiences designed like a play. All other humans and other creations surrounding you have met together to make up the characters of your drama and/or play. You chose all the members of your cast for the value each relationship offers for the acceleration of your Soul's evolution.

As an actor, you can utilize the guidelines provided within this book to help you discover the importance of taking your power back. Each technique presented provides you with sufficient information to assist you to reach specific goals. There will be no need to understand all the details about each technique before it works. Your Soul Self (High Self) will assist you in meeting the goals that can improve your well-being and joy.

As you make the decision to purchase and read this book, keep in mind, that in addition to reading the words of Amma, you will be required to apply what you already know is important. Then you can insert these new procedures (outlined in this book) to help you reach the goal of becoming the powerful, loving, healthy being you were destined to be.

An important step in your success is to keep an open mind and know "You Are In Charge and Can Change Anything In Your Life, Anything That Needs Changing." Your constant source of guidance for making meaningful changes will come from within as you tune into your Soul Self (High Self) and listen to guidance flowing from your heart center. Amma will help you understand you were created from Love and that Love is the most powerful force within the Universe.

Then you will discover you came to Earth with a guidance system purposely designed and controlled by your genetic codes. That system is called deoxyribonucleic acid (DNA). According to Amma these basic building blocks of the DNA contain ENCODEMENTS. You can come to understand there are two major types of encodements (natural and artificial). Together these encodements influence and in some manner control the many functions of all your energy bodies including your physical, mental, emotional and many spiritual bodies.

You will gradually begin to gain a better understanding that you have an option to seek spiritual help to repair, remove, and add new encodements to your control system. These available changes can improve your guidance systems and provide you with a more accurate control of all of your many energy patterns and activities. The injunction "You Must Ask to Receive" indicates there are spiritual assistants (encodement technicians and other spiritual beings) just waiting to respond to your requests. As you learn to take advantage of their help and live from the heart as opposed to living from the mind, you can discover the ability to resolve any imbalance that has caused you pain and suffering during this and other lifetimes.

Once you have succeeded in making contact with your Soul Self (High Self) and encodement technician's for assistance, then believe and know positive change will become very evident. Once these spiritual assistants (a multidimensional part of you) have responded to your requests, and those requests have been met, there will be a need for an acclimation (adjustment) period to download the changes. The length of the adjustment period may vary depending on the magnitude of the changes. In addition, you may discover a need for additional healing energies, more sleep, and a dedication towards self-discipline as the new you evolves.

Throughout your life activities on Earth, within the illusionary world of duality, make sure you apply the concept that what you think and add energy to, you create. Every thought is a creation. Thus to make a lasting change there will also be a need to clear out all malfunctional(malfunctioning) thoughts, false beliefs, negative crystallized emotions and other undesirable patterns stored anywhere within your body. That clearing process will also involve the removal of artificial encodements that serve no useful purpose. Then you may request new natural encodements be installed to empower your Spiritual Self and resolve any perceived need.

As you evolve to become the new you, realize how important is the injunction to avoid all forms of fear. Just know all forms of fear such as tension, worry, anxiety and stress destroy—while the emotion and energy of Love builds and can help create the new you. As you implement the concepts of Amma within this book, you will discover the power of Love. There is no value in becoming entrapped in any form of fear, because there is no-thing to fear, anywhere within the Universe. Amma will help you understand how important self-Love is.

May you gain new insights, as I have, from reading Cathy Chapman's new book, *The Heart: Doorway to Power*. Also, remember her first book containing information from Amma is entitled *Change Your Encodements, Your DNA, Your Life*. Each book contains many helpful insights and procedures for assisting your spiritual evolution.

Robert Pettit, PhD. April 2011

The Heart Doorway to Your Power

Questioning Amma

What Is My Power and Where Is It Located?

Precious Ones, it is good to be here with you.

For those who are new, you know me. I am your mother. I am Amma, the Divine Mother. I am the Divine Mother of the divine mothers. I Am the mother of those known as Quan Yin or Mother Mary or Isis or any of the divine mothers.

I am the feminine aspect of God in this world of duality. I come through this one known as Cathy Chapman and share messages with you. I come through others and share different messages. I work with people as they are, with the energy they have, and in the culture they are in.

I could come through two different people at exactly the same time, sending the same energy, and you would hear the same message expressed in two different ways. The energy I send is interpreted by the individual through the beliefs and experiences of the one receiving the messages.

This is my primary message to you—you are Love Incarnate and there is nothing but Love. You were created from Love, you are incarnated upon this planet, and that makes you Love Incarnate. What you are doing in this incarnation is discovering the Love that you are—and therein is the "secret" to your power.

Cathy Chapman: Amma, you've mentioned power several times in your messages to me. May we begin a discussion of power, what it is, and how to use it?

Amma: Of course, Dear One. Begin the conversation. What would you most like to know?

Cathy: First, what exactly is power?

Amma: Power, very simply, is the energy which is used to manifest from pure potential.

Cathy: Wow! There's a great deal contained in that definition. Don't we all manifest from pure potential?

Amma: Yes, everyone does. The fact that you are able to do so demonstrates how powerful you are. You manifest every part of your lives.

Cathy: You have said, I have said, and I hear it from everywhere, that we create our own reality. That is manifesting, is it not?

Amma: Yes, it is.

Cathy: It seems to me we've done a rather poor job of it all! Why would we create pain and suffering for anyone, including ourselves?

Amma: Let me approach this from several angles.

First, big picture/little picture or macrocosm/microcosm: Parents put certain restrictions on their children. They will tell a child when to go to bed, what to eat, when to eat, when to cross the street, when not to cross the street, and so on. The child frequently rebels at such restrictions. The child wants to do what s/he wants, when s/he wants. The child doesn't understand why there are these limitations.

The child becomes a parent and puts similar restrictions on his or her child. Why? Because the former "child" has grown up and is now aware of the "big picture."

There is an aspect of you that knows "the big picture." This aspect of yourself knows exactly what you wanted to accomplish in this lifetime. You planned the whole thing. You planned your lifetime down to the minute energy structures called encodements. They were placed within your energy body to assist you in receiving the exact experiences you wanted to have available to you.

You made this plan before you came to Earth. You knew exactly what you wanted to do, how you wanted to do it, and with whom you wanted to do it. Some of you made the decision to leave various options open in certain areas of your life. You wanted to experience as much as you could and discover the myriad possibilities life held for you.

Most of the inhabitants of this planet planned things very specifically. You decided if you made a particular choice, you would go in one direction. If, however, you made another choice, you would go down a different avenue. You made plans, and provided options, for the various crossroads in your life.

You left "Home" and are now here. When you left "Home," you were an infinite being who knew exactly what you were going to do and why. When you came to the "microcosm" on Earth, your current incarnation, or whatever you wish to call this experience, you "took on" the role needed for this Earth experience. The role was you, an infinite being, now experiencing limitation and powerlessness.

Think of it.

You had the experience of yourself as an infinite being in every way. Can you imagine the expansiveness of that infinity? Of course not! How can limitation experience lack of limitation? You, an infinite being, decided to become limited to experience, to taste, to sample what living life with limitation would be like.

To be truly limited, you entered into a body that couldn't even turn over by itself. You entered a body that could not find food unless it was put into your mouth. Even a newborn panda, no bigger than an acorn, can crawl up its mom and find the milk. You, as a newborn, couldn't do anything but cry, kick your legs, move your arms, and excrete. You could eat only if someone gave you the food.

You went from being limitless and infinite to having that knowledge and experience wiped away…then you entered a limited, powerless body. From the very beginning of your incarnation, you experienced limitation.

Cathy: Why couldn't we have come in with our power?
Amma: You could have, but you chose not to. That wasn't in your plan. You wanted to experience this world, this life, with limits.

You, a limitless, infinite being wanted to experience this life as a limited being. You are experiencing life in a way you could not have done as an infinite being. An infinite being cannot experience limitation unless that being constructs another reality, another world.

Cathy: A couple of weeks ago I watched a DVD called "The Thirteenth Floor." It was about a group of computer programmers who created a virtual world. They put themselves in it. They each experienced something totally different in their virtual world from the world they were in.
Amma: That particular movie is a wonderful analogy for what you each have done in this world. You, a limitless, infinite being, created a "virtual" world in which you experience something you are not.

Just as in the movie, the "people" in the virtual world experienced themselves as real. Each person experiences his or herself as real. There is very little "real" about you. Your body is not real, which means your illnesses are not real. The houses you live in are not real. Your clothes are not real. Your job is not real. The people around you are not real.

You created everything for this experience of limitation.

Cathy: The people around me aren't real? How can that be?
Amma: They appear real to you, but that is only an illusion.

You interact with them, these illusions of yours, in the way you need them to fulfill your goal for this lifetime. They simply play a role for you. They are no more real than you are. You are

Cathy Chapman

infinite. Those who play these roles are infinite. Notice the words in that sentence…they are playing a role, as you are.

Every part of you is manufactured, except for the aspect of consciousness which walks around in this "virtual world" you have created so wonderfully. Even the small aspect of consciousness is not "really" you. You are "really" an infinite, powerful, limitless being having an experience of limitation in your creation. People, including yourself, walk around believing you know someone. You have no idea who anyone is. You don't even know who you are—and I'm laughing joyfully as I say this.

You think you need me or another god. You do not. You are an infinite being. You need nothing outside of yourself. You are an aspect of me. I am within you.

Cathy: I feel as if I'm communicating with you right now. I am, am I not?

Amma: No, you are communicating with yourself. You think of me as other than you because you are afraid of claiming your power as an infinite being. You do this, as do all channels, because they find it more comfortable to have someone or something come through them rather than admit or accept that the energy coming in is truly what they are. Their consciousness, the part "channeling," is an aspect of who they are.

Of course, they can only channel a small part of themselves. The infinite is much more than any limited being can channel. Just putting the energy into words adds limitation to the energy you are receiving. The energy is infinite. When you interpret it, you put limitation to it. In other words, you give it a body, just as you limited yourself by creating for yourself a body.

Part of the limitation you've given yourself is seen in the fear you have that others will not accept your words, that they will berate you. You came from a background of strict religiosity. You have moved from those bindings into spirituality. You continue to experience vestiges of your "bindings" in the fear that you will be rejected by others.

The reason you have not been able to "channel" as you once did is because your Soul Self, that part of you that did not take on limitation, says it is now time for you to accept your power. (*Cathy had created the illusion of being ill and not doing public channeling.*) That aspect of yourself, that of which you are an infinitesimal part, has put this part of your if/then equation, one of your crossroads to another option, in motion.

Note how you "channel" now.

Cathy: I sit down at the computer and ask questions. I write down what comes to me. Some of what comes to me is triggered by what I'm learning in my own personal studies. That's when I wonder if I'm really "channeling" or if I'm making it all up. When I'm with a client, they ask a question, and I say what comes to me. The information seems to come from a place beyond me. Even when I'm expanding on things I've learned, the information seems to come from a place other than from me.

Amma: You are tapping into your Soul Self, what many call the Higher Self. You are tapping into the limitless, infinite You. This is the You guiding and directing your experience on this planet.

Cathy: That means I am limitless, here on this Earth?

Amma: Back to the analogy of parents limiting their children...you are limitless and you are not. You are limitless because you are an infinite being who is governing or managing all that is happening. You are limited because that aspect of yourself, the part you call "Cathy," which you chose to be limited, is limited. Your Soul Self is managing all that is happening in this lifetime. Your Soul Self has the "script," "the program," the plan you developed before you incarnated. Your Soul Self is the one directing or managing the plan you made before you entered into limitation.

Cathy: That means my Soul Self has all the power.

Amma: Yes, your Soul Self has the power because you chose that. You chose to re-learn certain things, experience certain things, and your Soul Self is making sure that happens. Your Soul Self is at the controls of the computer game.

That is what happens to everyone who incarnates on this planet. Even those you believe have great powers still have certain limitations. They have greater access to the awareness and knowledge of their power. They have greater knowledge of how to use their power. They are experiencing what it is they want to experience. If you have contact with one of these beings, it is because that is how you planned this life experience. If you decided before incarnation that you would meet one of these less limited beings, your Soul Self makes sure it happens.

Cathy: Does this mean that I, we, don't have any power?
Amma: This is where we go to the microcosm/macrocosm. Your Soul Self has all the power. Your Soul Self knows the big picture, what you wanted to experience and how you wanted to experience it. Your Soul Self has the plan with all the if/then equations. You, on this Earth plane, have power according to how you planned it.

Cathy: Am I limited to the if/then equations that I planned before incarnation?
Amma: You are asking that question from the perspective of a limited, finite being. You were (and are) an infinite, limitless being when you made the plans. There are an infinite number of if/then equations. There are equations to cover every possibility.

Cathy: If my Soul Self has all the power, does that mean that I don't have any power?
Amma: Again, you are asking that question from the perspective of a limited, finite being. "Cathy Chapman," is not who you are. The one you call "Cathy" is made up, not real. The "real" you, if you want to use that term, is the one that is your Soul Self.

Let's go back to the analogy of a two year old living in this world (speaking as if the illusion is real)...does a two year old have power? Yes, a limited amount. The parent, however, has most of the power. A two year old can decide to obey or not to obey, to eat or not to eat. As the child grows, the child will make more decisions independent of the parents. What the parents attempt to do is teach the child how to live in the world with its rules and regulations.

The parents want the child to know that if s/he sticks a finger in a flame, pain will result. Most parents want this learning to occur without actual pain. Parents will "child-proof" a house. When the child has learned not to stick paper clips in the electrical plug, the caps come off. The child learns how the rules work and can decide, from his or her own sense of power, whether to obey the rules or only follow particular ones. The child learns to make up his or her own rules.

As the child grows and develops, s/he learns that being nice will bring more friends. Being "too" nice, or letting people walk all over you, leads to pain. There is a "happy medium" between having personal boundaries no one can penetrate and having no boundaries at all.

As the individual grows, s/he learns that certain thoughts, certain actions, certain beliefs make life easier or more difficult. S/he learns that doing things in a certain way feels more powerful than doing, believing, thinking, feeling in other ways. The individual may learn that s/he has greater access to intuition if s/he focuses on the heart rather than the throat. The individual may learn to "travel" to distant areas by teleporting or in traveling within consciousness.

These experiences give the appearance of power. In fact, your experiences are limited by your Soul Self, your limitless, infinite self who is enjoying watching the experience that you, pretending to be a limited being, are having.

You and your Soul Self are one. The "you" in the illusion has forgotten this Truth. The persona doesn't remember or experience the Oneness. Your Soul Self is the Oneness.

The short answer is: Yes, you have complete power on one level, your infinite level. No, you do not have complete power on your finite level. However, you are learning about power! As you learn about the power that is yours, and how to use it, you believe you have tremendous power. The fact is that you as a limited being do not have total power. Your Soul Self does. You are learning how to use the limited power that you, the infinite being, have allowed yourself to have as a limited being. You experience yourself as powerful; yet, in actuality, as your incarnated self, you do not have unlimited power.

Back to the movie you mentioned earlier, each of the characters in the computer game grew and developed according to the program of the game. They thought they had power. They were, however, limited—as it is with you. Each incarnated being chooses to learn about power and how to use it during his or her particular human existence. Some will experience greater expansiveness than others will. It is all in the plan, and no one is better than anyone else.

Cathy: Will we ever be able to access our total power?

Amma: Not as an incarnated being. You will always experience some limitation because it wouldn't be fun anymore in this earthly experience. If you had all your power, you would not be any different from your "real" self, your Soul Self. This planetary "game" you planned so thoroughly would end and then you would choose something new to explore.

Cathy: As I've done the encodement work and changed so much of my life, I feel more powerful.

Amma: Yes, you do. You have learned to access more of the limited amount of power you have available to you. As a human being in this human experience, you are learning, as it were, the rules of the Earth game. You are learning how things may go more smoothly. You are also learning that you, and everyone on this planet, have within you energy structures that are doorways to your power. Your power is hidden where you were least likely to look…within you!

You have learned through encodement work that you can change many aspects of your life. In your psychology language, you may say that you are no longer victim to certain happenings. You now know a very powerful way in which you can change patterns in your life. Before you knew about encodements, you could change but not as quickly. Now you can change even more quickly.

Before you knew about encodements, you did meditations to clear the chakras. Now you can do encodement work which will also clear the chakras. You have discovered you have the power to clear the chakras even more quickly. Your increased knowledge and use of your power comes with your increased awareness.

All these possibilities were planned. Your Soul Self has been directing it. You, the persona, haven't had to do anything except follow your inner direction. Even when you didn't think you were following your inner knowing, the plan was still unfolding. Experiencing the results of not following your inner knowing is also part of the script.

When I say you do not have power, I am speaking on a comparative basis. A wave, even if it were 30 feet high, is still only a very small portion of the ocean. Your ocean is so vast that you have divided it into sections and given each a name so you can refer to them more easily. The fact is that there is only one ocean dotted by landmasses. One wave, no matter how small or how large, is only a small portion of that ocean.

Your power in this human incarnation is no more than a small portion of the power you have as an infinite being. You are part of consciousness. Consciousness is infinite. You have access to the infinite. Your power within the infinite consciousness, when you incarnate, becomes individualized and, thereby, finite. The ocean, as vast as it is, is finite. You as an incarnated being, no matter how much you accessed your infinite power, would still be finite. Others may see you differently because they view you through the eyes of believing they have greater limitation. In this world in which you live, you have different experiences of power. The most powerful among you, as an incarnated being, still does not have the power to create a star.

In your life you learn about the power of a human. When you learned to crawl, you felt the power of being able to move where you wanted. You took great delight in exploring your world.

Your parents became concerned you would hurt yourself and placed you in a playpen. You began to walk. You were then able to go outside and play by yourself. What power and freedom you experienced when you could ride your bike wherever you wanted! Then you could drive. Remember that feeling of power and freedom?

As you grew, you also learned about relationship with others and with yourself. You learned about emotions and feelings. In your adulthood, you learned that emotions were energy. If you used this powerful energy in one way, you felt depleted and powerless. If you used it in another way, you felt powerful. You learned how the energy of anger, with all its power, could destroy if you did not manage it. If you learned to channel the anger in specific ways, you could use that energy to move you forward and accomplish many things.

When you became aware of the energy system, you learned more about energy. You learned how thoughts and feelings affect your energy field. Remember when you discovered the peace of staying in your heart, the power of staying in your heart? Your research scientists have demonstrated with their instruments the power you can access by staying in your heart. You discovered that power is hidden in your heart.

There are thousands of books on each of these topics.

Cathy: I'm confused because I had come to believe that I am powerful. I'm not able to manifest things out of thin air, but I feel powerful in many ways.

Amma: This is the paradox. You are powerful in many ways. When you are able to manifest out of thin air, then you will come to know, in some small way, how powerful you truly are. You believe you are powerful because you are so much happier than you ever have been in this lifetime. You believe you are powerful because you have freed yourself from most of the bonds of emotion dragging you down. You have done much work on changing limiting belief systems. These have given you the experience of power.

However, this experience of power is no more than a drop of water compared to the ocean of power you actually are...and remember, the ocean is limited.

Cathy: Can I, can we, experience even more power?
Amma: Yes, of course.

Cathy: What must we do to experience more power?
Amma: It is fairly simple. Note that I did not say easy.

First, you must recognize you are an infinite, unlimited being having a finite, limited experience. You must come to believe that all you were taught about limitation is false. Yes, you can learn to walk on water. Yes, you can learn to teleport. Yes, you can learn to live without food, water, even money. You can, Dear One, learn to manifest exactly what you need and want at the time you need and want it.

All this you can do under the direction of your Soul Self.

Second, you must be willing to recognize that everything you see is illusion. It is your own construct. Your infinite self, your Soul Self, constructed everything, even those in relationship with you. You are not separate from your Soul Self. You are a manifestation of your Soul Self. You are no more separate than the wave is from the ocean.

Third, you must reclaim the energy used to create all you have created for this life experience.

Fourth, rejoice in all you have done from the aspect of your limited self to the aspect of your Soul Self. You are indeed a magnificent, powerful being.

Cathy: I get confused. Sometimes you say I have no power and other times you say that I have power.
Amma: Oh, and fifth, quit trying to figure it all out. Simply accept. Your experience as a limited, finite being is an illusion, which you, as a limitless, infinite being, created. You cannot understand, as a limited being living in this wondrous microcosm, all the questions which arise from what I have told you.

Cathy: Don't try to figure it all out? You've given me such an inquiring mind. I use it often. I enjoy figuring things out.

Amma: This wondrous creation you live in just is. It is as you created it. By the way, you gave yourself that wondrous inquiring mind.

Cathy: As I created it? What about everyone else?

Amma: If everyone created their world exactly the same way, everything would be the same. Everyone would view the world in the same way. As a therapist doing family therapy, you are familiar with how each family member can view one particular event in different ways. Even the words may be different. Three members of a family can vociferously claim that another said, "We'll go to the beach on Thursday" and two others will just as forcefully claim that the words were, "We will not go to the beach on Thursday." Who is right?

There is no right or wrong. They each perceived, heard, experienced exactly what they needed to experience for their own life path. This path, these experiences, are created by you in the form of your Soul Self.

You have read about court cases where three impartial observers saw three different things. Are they all lying? No. They each saw what happened from the filters of their own beliefs, own perceptions, own experiences, their own creations.

Since those filters, beliefs and perceptions are different from one to another, what they "saw" is also different. Yes, there can be similarities. Yes, there can often be total agreement. Then you have a newspaper story that all agreed that one person raped or killed someone and, years later, DNA evidence says that person could not possibly have done it.

What happened? Again, people viewed things from their own filters consisting of their perceptions and beliefs.

Cathy: How does power fit into this?

Amma: Power is contained in each creation, from the tiniest atomic structure to the largest mountain. You, your Soul Self, is the one who devised this creation. You are an infinitely powerful, limitless being…not in your human form but in your true self, your true essence.

Using analogies: You are the drop of water in the ocean. You are the leaf on the redwood tree. You are the tiniest particle in the molecule that makes up the chair you are sitting on. You are the spark of consciousness manifested on Earth by the infinite, limitless being called by many names. You are *a part* of "that"…not *apart* from "that."

Only in this form you presently experience, the Cathy Chapman form, are you limited…and that is only in the belief systems of your mind.

Recently you were at a workshop in which two of the participants could not "see" the hotel on the street where it was. One of them told you that the hotel "disappeared." They looked and looked, drove and drove. No matter how many times they went down the street, the hotel…where they had been the day before…was gone. Then they "found" it.

Did both of them just not see the hotel? Were they both that unobservant? You know these two women. Is that typical of them?

Cathy: No, it's not typical. They are both very powerful people. What happened?

Amma: They were displaying their creative power!

Those of you on this journey to discovering the power that you really are, the truth about who you really are, are having experiences of creating and un-creating. They experienced, as you have at times, the true "unreality" of the world. When things disappear and you find them in the same place you looked ten times, you attribute it to lack of observation. Sometimes it is certainly not observing. Many times it is your Soul Self "un-creating" something so that you can experience how things are not real.

Remember your friend who had a 12-year-old stranger take her gas cap from her car while she was pumping gas?

Cathy Chapman

Cathy: Yes, he told her that he would give it back to her for some money. She wouldn't give it to him and he wouldn't give her the gas cap. The next morning she found the gas cap on the seat of her car. She was amazed. She accepted with wonder and amazement the gas cap reappearing because she knew things like that could happen.

There was another incident where I had given my niece a small crystal. It "disappeared." She found it sitting right smack in the middle of the entryway to the bathroom. Because we had heard of such things, we attributed it to the crystal playing games with us.

Then there is the friend who left her cell phone charger in a hotel in Europe. When she got back home to Texas, she dropped all her suitcases at the bottom of the stairs and went to bed. When she woke up the next morning, the phone charger was sitting on her counter. Nothing had been unpacked.

Amma: All of you, in the form of your Soul Selves, were playing games with yourselves. The game was and is "Discovering the Truth of Reality." The reality is that you are limitless, powerful and a creator. The fullness of that power is contained within your Soul Self, but you are not separate from your Soul Self, no more than the wave is separate from the ocean. You are One yet with language being what it is, we must speak in duality. When events of "disappearing" and "re-appearing" occur, note that you are being shown that the things you have are not real. They are illusion, and wonderfully created illusion.

Cathy: What about the people in my life? Are they illusion?
Amma: How you perceive them is your creation. You do not have the ability as a human being to see them as they truly are.

Cathy: My brother Chris, his death, the pain I feel at his loss even years later, that is illusion?
Amma: Yes, Dear One. No matter what you experience, no matter the horrors or the amount of pain. It is illusion. That is not who you are or who he was and is. He served a purpose for you that you created. He had his own purpose which he created. His purpose

and anyone else's purpose, even family and clients, are none of your business. The only part that is your business is their purpose for you. You are the one who created them for that purpose.

Even with all the pain surrounding your brother, would you rather to never have had him?

Cathy: No, I loved him. Is that love an illusion?

Amma: No, love is not an illusion. Love is that from which you were made. Love is the very building block of all creation. With Love, you can create anything.

Cathy: What about pain and suffering? Is that from Love also?

Amma: You do not know what Love truly is. Love is not an emotion or a feeling. Love is a substance from which all is made. All that occurs in the illusion of your life, the play of your life, is made from Love. It does not feel like Love to you. When you leave this wondrous body of yours, and it is wondrous no matter what condition it is in, you will know and understand all there is about how things work on the created level.

Cathy: Fear is Love?

Amma: I have said that fear is "not Love." I used that more as a point/counter-point to better elucidate what I wanted to say. I can now build upon that statement.

Let me give another analogy. When you are teaching children numbers, you do not tell them there are negative numbers. You let them become familiar and comfortable with the concept of whole numbers. You don't even mention positive and negative numbers.

As they acquire knowledge and experience you introduce the concept of negative numbers. Still later, you introduce rational and irrational numbers.

There is only one energy and that energy is Love. Everything you experience is a vibration of Love. Using the numbers analogy, some vibration is labeled as "positive" and other vibration is labeled as "negative." There are no positive and negative vibrations. There are only varying vibrations of the same substance.

In actuality, fear is an aspect of Love because there is only Love.

When you want to change colors for the font on your document, you go to a particular place that has various colors. If you do not see the color you want there, you can click on another button, which takes you to a color wheel. All the colors are within that color wheel. They are all part of the one. Each color is simply a different frequency. They are all of the same energy.

The teachings I am giving you on power are about working with the various frequencies and vibrations of the energy I call Love. I will give you suggestions on managing the power of your bodies (physical, mental, emotional, spiritual) living in this world, which you have created, and various methods to come to know who you truly are in the fullness of your power.

Cathy: Will you teach more about encodements?
Amma: Yes, I will teach more about encodements. I will teach about the various creations that humans make through their many institutions…be they financial, religious, governmental or corporate. I will teach about the power contained within your bodies and how to tap into and use the energy present.

What I teach can be found somewhere else in this wondrous world of yours. I will teach little, if anything, that is new but I will package it in a different manner. I will discuss how power in your world seems to have gone awry and what can be done if you wish to change it. This will be a fun conversation.

Cathy: Will you teach us how to come in touch with the powerful beings we truly are?
Amma: Yes, I will. I will teach you how to become more powerful in all areas of your life. First, you must learn how to use the

power you have in this four-dimensional world of height, length, width and time. Then I will talk about accessing your power contained within your unlimited, infinite self.

Cathy: This will be quite a journey.

Amma: Yes, it will. For those following you on the journey, they will find it necessary to establish communication with their own Soul Self...if they have not already done so. Begin to experience the energy, the power, which is beyond this finite world you live in. Ask for assistance from your Soul Self to learn all that is within your script to learn. You may ask your encodement technicians to align your encodements for learning about and accessing your true infinite power.

Not everyone will want to do so. Not everyone planned to do so. Those who will not, did not write this into their script for this incarnation. Those who do not "get around to it" or do not do the work needed, simply planned it this way. There is nothing wrong in staying where you are. There is no better or best. There only Is.

My blessings to you, Dear One, and to all who read these words. My love is enfolding each person who reads and hears my words. I am Amma, the Divine Mother of divine mothers and I am your mother.

———•·•———

The Heart Source and Heart Hologram

Dear Ones, the information that follows was begun in 2006. Since that time, I have given you crucial information about your energy field that is of utmost importance. This new information is contained in an email course I asked this one to make available to as many people as possible for as little cost as possible.

Those of you who use modern technology may access that course at www.AmmaTheDivineMother.com. There is an English and Spanish version at this time. This course will come in your email every day. Although I'm going to give you directions for activating important energy structures within your energy body, the email course, also in book form, assists you in working with these structures daily.

As you practice the incremental steps given in the daily course, you can ensure that the Heart Source is fully activated within you. You want to learn to live from your Heart Source. Why?

The Heart Source is a multi-dimensional structure activating the potential within the front and back of your heart center and the front and back of your brow center. Living from your Heart Source will assist you in doing the following:

- Stay centered and grounded.
- Activate your intuition more fully.
- Assist you in discerning the truth of information.
- Connect you with multi-dimensional information.

You must learn to live from your Heart Source if you wish to be in your power. Although I recommend you imprint your Heart Source through the five-week daily process contained in the daily program, I give it to you here as it is a necessary aspect of yourself for your re-membering your power as an infinite being.

The Heart Source

You form the Heart Source through the following steps:

1. Enter into the back of your heart center.
2. Enter into the front of your heart center.
3. Enter into the front of your brow center.
4. Enter into the back of your brow center.
5. Connect your heart center with your brow center with a beam of light moving through your pranic tube from the heart center to the brow.
6. Move that beam of light up to the Center of the Universe (don't worry where that is).
7. Move the light to the center of the earth.

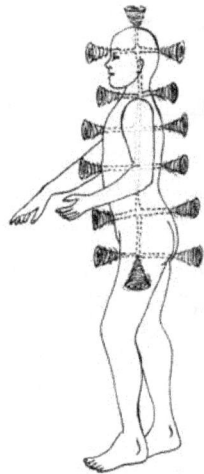

The daily course on accessing your power gives you specific directions on how to do this and fully activate it within you. You will also learn how to live from and use your Heart Source. The daily course is the perfect accompaniment to this book.

The Heart Hologram

You already have the Heart Hologram. Since I first gave the Heart Hologram to the world during a session in Japan in 2005, it was transmitted throughout the planet in viral fashion.

Cathy Chapman

Once someone with the Heart Hologram connects with another person in a heart-to-heart manner, the Heart Hologram was immediately transmitted to the other. There was no permission required as the Heart Hologram is a new part of your energy structure. It's contained within the heart chakra.

Once the Heart Hologram is present, there is access to multidimensional awareness. Awareness of life begins to change subtly. Just as everyone has a heart chakra, but not everyone uses it, the same is true for the Heart Hologram. When you are within your heart, your Heart Hologram is active. When you are in your Heart Source, your Heart Hologram is even more active. There will be more information about the Heart Hologram at a later time. Using it will be important in Spiritual LoveFare, the returning of the dark to the Light…but that is another book. (*Information about Spiritual Lovefare is found at* www.SpiritualLovefare.com—*Cathy. You can join the Spiritual Lovefare Team at this web site.*)

For those of you who can "see" with your inner eye, look into your heart center. Do you see a moving geometric structure? That is the Heart Hologram. Are you surprised it is there? If you have been reading my words of love, or the words of love of other beings, you were given the Heart Hologram.

If you are not sure you have the Heart Hologram, simply ask for it. Just say, "Amma, please give me the Heart Hologram." Now tone "Om" three times, or more if you wish.

Once you have the Heart Hologram you strengthen it in yourself and another every time you connect with him or her heart-to-heart. If you want to do spiritual work while waiting in line, or on the bus, train, plane, or just waiting…connect with those you see heart-to-heart. Now chant "Om" three times into their heart. You may do the chanting within the deepness of your mind and heart.

You may connect with anyone you see in person, through photographs, even in movies or television, and strengthen their Heart Hologram. All the babies being born have the Heart Hologram. It is now part of the energy structure. Although you may strengthen another's Heart Hologram, it is their responsibility to use it.

The information in this book was transmitted to you several years ago. There are some changes I'm asking this one to make to update the information. Much has happened and much has been given over these few years.

It is time now for this information to be disseminated as widely as possible.

My blessings surround you as you work through this information. You will feel downloads of energy at various times. Just relax and enjoy. You may ask your encodement technicians to adjust your encodements to allow you to assimilate more easily this information as well as the energies coming into the planet.

Go to www.AmmaTheDivineMother.com if you do not know about encodements. There you can explore and play with the information. This one I speak through writes in a "linear" rather than "circular" manner as given in the book *Change Your Encodements, Your DNA, Your Life*.

Enjoy the information contained. My blessings enfold you continually.

———

Beginning to Understand Power

Dear Ones, please read this information from your Heart Source.

The Heart Source

You form the Heart Source through the following steps:

1. Enter into the back of your heart center.
2. Enter into the front of your heart center.
3. Enter into the front of your brow center.
4. Enter into the back of your brow center.
5. Connect your heart center with your brow center with a beam of light moving through your pranic tube from the heart center to the brow.
6. Move that beam of light up to the Center of the Universe (don't worry where that is).
7. Move the light to the center of the earth.

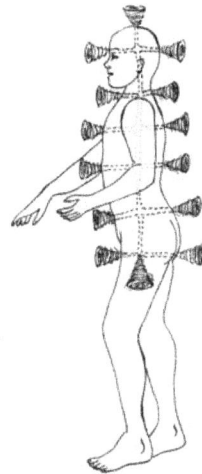

This discussion about power will contain some review of the encodement system and its purpose. Those of you who are not familiar with encodements, or who enjoy a more linear presentation, will find this very beneficial. Those of you who believe you know a great deal about encodements, know there is new information here.

Let me begin by reiterating Who You Truly Are. You are an aspect of a limitless, infinite energy many people call God. You could also be called an aspect of the pure creative force, universal energy, pure potential. As an aspect of that creative force, you have all, and I do mean all, of the capabilities of the infinite Oneness.

I am unable to speak with precision about what happens because my words will always be in duality since that is where you are—in duality. That is the nature of incarnating upon this delightful planet you call Earth. Know that the truth is much more wondrous, much more beautiful, much more complex and, yes, much simpler than you are reading.

Let's go back to the words "aspect of a limitless, infinite energy." You not only are an aspect of, you are limitless and infinite. You are all wise, all knowing. That is what you are in the "reality" of who you are.

Move into your Heart Source if you are not already there. Now go deeper into your heart center. Breathe in and out of your heart center. Allow your consciousness to expand beyond your body. Now beyond the room. Beyond the building. Beyond the block. Beyond the city. Keep expanding. Notice what you experience.

Another exercise for you: From that expanded place, ask a question you have wondered about. If you are involved in the healing profession and have wanted to know how to heal or work with someone who has multiple sclerosis (MS), ask "What is the first thing I need to do to work with someone with MS?" Continue asking follow-up questions. (You might want to have a tape recorder with you to speak aloud what you are receiving.) Simply begin speaking or writing whatever comes. Allow the information to flow.

If you are an engineer, ask about the best way to solve an engineering problem. If you are a teacher, ask about the best way to teach a subject to someone with a particular learning disability.

What information came to you? Did you allow yourself to expand your awareness? Did you allow yourself to speak or write the information that came into your mind? Did you allow the information to come into your mind?

If you did not receive any information, you now know you believe you are unable to do so. Note that I said you "believe" you are unable to receive information. You are a limitless, infinite being who has access to all the knowledge in the universe...and beyond. The more you believe that, the more information you will be able to access.

You may now ask, "Why can't I access all the information? Why can't I exercise miraculous powers now?" The answer is very simple, "You would not be experiencing the incarnation you designed if you suddenly experienced the fullness of your infinite ability."

Not being able to access all your power is not a punishment for being upon this planet. It was a choice you made to experience life as you are experiencing it. Let me emphasize that again. Your life as you are living it is your choice. You planned this and you planned it perfectly.

All this to say that the first thing you need to impress upon your mind is you are a limitless, infinite being. Think of all the movies you have seen of people with tremendous powers. Your writers have tapped into the knowledge of what it is that each of you is capable of doing. Yes, each of you has the capability of being what you would call a miracle worker. Why aren't you? Because that is not how "you" designed this life to this point.

An analogy would be helpful here. Before you came to this incarnation you planned this play of yours. (Remember the words from the one you call Shakespeare, "All the world's a stage. All men and women merely players.") You decided what you wanted to experience and to learn. You, in a sense, left a script "on the other side" which is being directed in every detail by your Soul Self.

Once you finished the script, you got together your "costuming." Costuming began with your encodements. You worked with the encodement technicians in minute detail about what it was you wanted to experience, learn (actually remember), achieve and do in this lifetime. You also stated the possibilities of what you might want to do and what you did not want to do. In every juncture of your life you had "equations" that stated, "If I did this, then I would next do this. If this happened, then this would happen."

An example: This one I am writing through (Cathy Chapman) had strong encodements for two different ways to learn about structure, discipline and freedom. No matter which path she took, she would have learned and experienced what she planned. However, depending upon which path she took, different other events, learning (remembering), would have occurred. Would you like to know what those two different paths were? You will be surprised.

One path was the one she took. She entered the convent for twenty years. To open up that path to her, she selected a being to be her mother who was deeply spiritual. Her mother's energy triggered for her the encodements regarding a structured religious path.

She also selected a being as a father who had the energy of the military. Her father's father was a general in the Air Force and she, herself, was born on an Air Force base while her own father was in the military.

Her "play" moved to the critical juncture of which path she would take. Would she enter the military or would she enter the convent? She did, by the way, consider the military.

What do these two paths have in common? Both are about structure, obedience and personal power. You may ask, "What about the spiritual part? Would she have channeled?"

First, know that each person is spiritual. Because of her mother, her spiritual encodements were awakened. With either path, she would have dynamically explored her spiritual path. Each path would have taken her beyond traditional Christianity. Each path would have taught her, pushed her, to examine the question of personal power in a structure where she had to take orders from someone.

Would she have channeled? Probably not. In fact, most likely, her life in this incarnation would be over. Those who have read her story know about the accident she later realized was when she had "planned" to leave this life—and didn't. The probability is she would have left this incarnation at that accident. She did not begin channeling until after this juncture.

Each of you has similar junctures in your life. Each one of you planned what you wanted to learn (remember) and the possibilities of how you would remember it. Some of you planned minutely this experience of the illusion of learning. Others of you had multiple possibilities. All of these were and are contained within your encodement structure.

You have access to tremendous power within your encodement structure. You can change these encodements. All changes are done in partnership with your Soul Self.

Let's now examine the types of encodements you have.

There are two major categories of encodements for the human: natural and artificial.

Natural Encodements

Of the natural encodements there are four types and purposes. Three are placed within you by the encodement technicians in agreement with you (the infinite being you are, your Soul Self) before incarnation. These encodements:

- Guide your path in the direction you planned before you incarnated…including the elaborate plan to convince yourself you are limited.

- Carry over what you call genetic information from the family of origin you chose to begin this illusion of your life. These can be called "generational encodements." They are still within the plan you constructed, but are separated here for clarity in working with them.

- Encodements placed by the encodement technicians that relate to other lifetimes…another fun way to play with illusion. Again, these encodements are placed within you to guide you in the direction of the path you planned. They are separated simply for ease in working with them.

- The last category of natural encodements includes those that the encodement technicians place within you at your request. This can be done on a Soul level (Soul Self) without your conscious knowledge or by you consciously asking. This is done to support your life path by making any adjustments necessary through your growth and development.

Natural encodements can be active or inactive. When you were conceived your active encodements generally related to the unfolding of your physical growth and the energy system (chakras, meridians, etc.) to support your growth. As you are well aware, most people spend about nine months within the womb of their birth mother. During this time what affects the mother affects the growing infant. Her thoughts and feelings originating from within her, and in reaction to those about her, have an effect upon your natural encodements (as well as her own). The energy from others around her also has an effect upon your natural encodements, depending upon how she handles their energy.

The energy from your mother can support, damage or alter your natural encodements. Her thoughts and feelings also support, damage or alter her own natural encodements. The same is true for you now. Your thoughts and feelings, both spontaneously originating from you and those in response to the energy coming from outside of yourself, will support, damage or alter your natural encodements.

Natural encodements have, as it were, a timetable in which they become active. You do not need the encodements for profession before you activate the encodements to crawl. Any of these encodements can be damaged, altered or delayed in their activation by how you process the energy around you. Please note that I said,

"How you process the energy." Your realization and ability to process energy from outside of yourself is the beginning of rediscovering your power.

Artificial Encodements

The second type of encodements is known as artificial encodements. These energy structures alter your energy in some way. They can interfere with natural encodements on the most basic level, or cause difficulties with the flow of energy in your chakras and meridians. Some people may refer to them as thought forms; however, there is a subtle difference between artificial encodements and thought forms. Not all thought forms produce artificial encodements, yet artificial encodements are the result of thought forms.

By thought forms, I'm referring to the energy produced by the thoughts, words and actions of another or yourself. A thought form from one person can have varying amounts of strength depending upon the intent and energy behind the thought form, as well as the vibration of other thought forms already present.

As an example: The thought, "I'll never succeed." If this thought is "new" to the individual (i.e., they rarely, if ever, have it and few, if any, have told them this is true) and is quickly dismissed by the individual, there is little power in the energy produced. It will quickly dissipate like the smoke from an extinguished match. The energy does not take form; therefore, there is no "thought form."

If, however, an individual has been told most of life s/he will never succeed, and comes to a task and says or thinks with fervor, "I'll never succeed!" this energy takes form and coalesces with the energy of similar thought forms. The new thought form builds upon the previous thought forms, anchoring that thought more fully into the individual.

The thought forms that enter into the individual are the ones that form artificial encodements, meaning they will alter the basic energy flow of the person. When this occurs, the flow of meridians and chakras is altered. The more energy attached to the thought form, the stronger the artificial encodement and the more drastic the change in the energy.

In the above example, if the parents, teachers, individual, society, and friends all tell someone s/he won't succeed, and the individual agrees with the statement by reinforcing the statement him/herself, the artificial encodement for not succeeding will be very strong.

Thought forms might not produce artificial encodements, but may damage or alter natural encodements. Thought forms may also de-activate or prevent natural encodements from activating "according to schedule." Altering, damaging, de-activating, or delaying activation of natural encodements can also occur with the influx of energy that does not produce the energy structures of thought forms.

Everything on the planet has encodements. Those with shorter life cycles (people, plants, animals, insects, fish, etc.) have more encodements than those with longer life cycles (minerals). The planet herself and all planets that "house" shorter life cycles have innumerable encodements.

I have spoken of the encodement structure as if all is separate. Of course, all is one. All encodements interact with every other encodement. If you have a string of lights connected one to another in a direct line, when one light goes out, the string of lights, depending upon the wiring, may be extinguished at that point. If the lights are strung together in such a way that one light out will not affect the rest, the other lights stay on but the entire string has a diminished output of light. Imagine now that every light is connected to every other light. When one light is dimmer, another light is affected in some way. It is so with encodements and your energy field but in a more complex manner. An alteration in one aspect of the Oneness has the illusion of altering the Oneness.

How are encodements related to meridians, chakras and the aura? Every energy structure has encodements. These basic energies form the energies of the chakras, meridians, aura and any other energy structure within you. The relationship between them is not linear, even if the explanation is linear.

The encodements are similar to the operating system of a computer. Your myriad of opportunities and choices for this lifetime are contained within your encodement system. There are encodements regarding your physical body as well as your energy bodies. When your encodement system is placed within the physical body, your encodements "unfold," as it were, as your physical body grows and develops. What happens to the growing physical body affects the encodements; and the encodements affect the growth of the physical body.

As both your physical body and encodement system unfold, so do your energy bodies. The development of the meridians is greatly affected by the union of the physical body and encodements. In addition, there are many other structures of the energy system including your central canal, core star, soul seat, tan tien, and many other wondrous structures. Although the aura is the final "part" of your energy structure, (remember I'm explaining something non-linear in a linear manner) it comes to its fullness when your spirit enters into the body.

All structures, physical and energetic, encodements and DNA, are enlivened in the true sense of the word when your spirit enters into the body. All structures, physical and energetic are affected when any one part of any structure is affected. There are many detailed writings on these various energy structures. If you wish to know more, please research the topic. Just know that whatever you read will be discussing the structures as if they are independent from the other parts of the body. This is, of course, because it is impossible to demonstrate the dynamic relationship of all anatomy, energy and physical, with the written word.

As you grew in your mother's womb, each of your bodies—physical and energy—interacted with your birth mother's bodies, physical and energy. What happened to her affected you. It affected your growth in the womb. It affected your DNA and your encodements. It affected every aspect of you. The interactions between you and your mother were dynamic in nature, not static. Her relationship with everyone and everything in her life affected her also. Since it affected her, it affected you. From the moment your body began its growth, it shifted and changed according to what happened to your birth mother.

You may say, "Yes, of course, I know this."

Dear Ones, I want you to *know* this to the depth of your being. Everything that affected your birth mother affected you. This was the plan you made. That is why you chose her and the family into which you were born. The beginning of your life plan began when the sperm entered the ovum! The energy system necessary for your life plan began to develop in the way you needed immediately upon conception. The energy of conception affected your encodements.

This collection of writings is about power. Your power in this lifetime began before you incarnated when you decided what it was you wanted to do this lifetime. *You* made those decisions. *You* developed your encodement structure. *You* developed the hardware and software of your play or movie here on this planet. *You,* yes, *You* decided what it was you would do, the possibilities you would have, and when you would make those choices.

When you incarnated, you "left" yourself. I say it this way because there is no other way to express it in words. An aspect of yourself incarnated and took on the role of the main player, your persona, in your play. The one now directing all the action is your Soul Self. Your Soul Self (You) knows what s/he (You) wanted to accomplish in this lifetime. Your Soul Self is arranging things so that events will occur exactly as needed.

Everything you do in your life interfaces with your encodement system. This material is written using a computer with an operating system. Overlaying the operating system is the word processing program. Although the words appear to be independent of the software, each stroke is supported by the software. So, too, with your life and your encodement structure. Each "stroke" of your life is supported by your encodement system.

There are also encodements for the rest of your energy structure. Encodements support your chakras, meridians and aura. In addition, there are many energy structures within each of those structures. Your energy structure is as varied and complex as the anatomy of your human body. For example, there are structures within chakras, chakras within chakras, and structures within those chakras. There are your major meridians and there are the smaller pathways from your meridians. This is similar to veins, arteries and capillaries in your circulatory system. There are numerous structures within your aura.

Let it suffice that there is a complex overall energy structure affecting every aspect of your physical body and your life. The greater detail of your knowledge, the more complex can be your methods of working with these structures. Then again, there are also simple ways to work with complexity. The methods we will discuss revolve around simplicity.

There will be little here that you have not heard in another form from someone else. If you have not heard it from someone on this planet, you may have a "remembering" of the truth of these words.

Where Your Power Hides

It has been said that the safest place to hide something is in plain view. The searcher will look in places well hidden. S/he will go to great lengths and much expense to find this thing of great value, and will not look in front of his/her nose.

In the case of power, the searcher rarely considers looking within. Even when acknowledging that power is within, the searcher will still look outward to books, movies, and others to find power. If the searcher can use these resources to "discover" the power residing within, the search is over!

The techniques I'm teaching are simply ways to assist you in discovering that you can move and change energy. Learning to move energy is one way you begin to experience how powerful you are. When you experience using your intent to move energy, and something happens within you, you become aware of your power. You become more comfortable with the Truth you are a powerful infinite being having a well-planned experience in this life.

What few people comprehend is that you intentionally hid your power. You may have heard the myth or analogy of drinking from the river of forgetfulness before you incarnated. To do what you wanted to do, you had to forget. When you take on a role in a play, you put aside who you "really" are and play the part.

The same is true here. You put aside who you really are, an infinitely powerful being, and play the part of a finite, powerless human. That's why you were born helpless. That's why you spent the first years of your life dependent upon someone to care for your every need. Those early years were devised to convince you that you had no power. A very successful plan, was it not?

During your early growth, encodements were activated according to a timetable specific to you. These were the encodements for certain developmental milestones—turning over, sitting up, crawling, standing, walking, and so on. Anyone who has watched more than one child develop can tell you there is a general range of when these so-called developmental tasks occur. When they take place in you, no matter how minor the task may seem, there is an effect upon your personal growth and development. That may sound simple but, in fact, your development and why it happens when it happens, is according to a complex plan you will find wondrous when you "re-discover" how it was accomplished.

Everyone reading these words is in a different stage of coming to awareness about who they truly are. Some of you are more aware than others. Some have tremendous awareness of their own power, so much awareness that they know these words are written by someone whose sole purpose for the reader's life is to give information or facilitate a change of some kind. Those truly aware of their own power realize they are reading something written by an aspect of themselves. They know that power is within them, not outside of them.

Others are searching for something or someone to assist them in knowing to the depths of their being there is no power outside of him or herself. What a paradox! You know on an intellectual level there is Oneness. This means there is no power outside of you, but you don't know how to reconnect with that power. You believe someone outside of you, which can't be there if there is Oneness, will give you that power. The paradox continues.

Then again, there are those who glance at this information and discard it with a snort. It simply was not in their plan to know it at this time. There are those who have read or heard some of the information and fear for their very souls. Others, whose plan was to be totally unaware of this information, never even saw this when it was right before their eyes. They truly did not see it.

Do you recognize many of your loved ones in the last paragraph? Know they are on their path and your job is not to contrive to move them in the direction you want them to go, even with the best of intentions. They are living their plan. Their Soul Self, even if they are not aware of a Soul Self, is in full control. Focus on your own path. Allow others their path, even if you believe that path is filled with pain.

The best way to discover your own power is to use your power. I'm going to begin with some simple exercises. Even though you may be well aware of these exercises, I will also explain and describe what happens energetically when you do them.

Let's begin by discussing the heart center. If you were to do nothing other than focus upon your heart center, you would have tremendous changes within your life. For those who are new to accessing your energy system, your heart center is in the center of your chest, just to the right of where the physical heart is said to be.

The heart center has a front and a back. You can enter the heart center from either direction. Imagine that the front and the back connect with the pranic tube in the general location of your spine.

The heart center is the transformational center of your energy system. It brings together the energy of your existence in the physical world with your connection to the spiritual world. In addition, when you enter the heart center from the front, you can access information regarding your present physical body and this lifetime. When you enter from the back, you can enter the space of infinity.

Experiment entering the heart center from both front and back.

When focusing on your heart center, you are able to stay grounded and can more easily access your intuition and higher senses (clairvoyance, clairaudience, clairsentience). As you focus on your heart center, you are able to temper the energy of your thoughts. When focusing on your heart center, information from your senses is interpreted from the energy of your heart center which has access to the energy of Oneness. When information is first interpreted by one of the lower chakras (referring to position, not to importance), the energy usually moves to the brain where there is a reaction based upon your past information and beliefs. The result is a constricting of the corpus callosum (a structure between the two sides of the brain). The constriction inhibits communication between the right and left sides of the brain.

Even if you have heard for years, "Stay in your heart center," commit yourself now to paying particular attention to living life from your heart center. A dedicated musician practices scales. A proficient golfer practices putting and driving. The spiritual master lives from the heart center, at minimum, and ultimately from the Heart Source. The basics are the building blocks for proficiency in any field.

When you focus on your heart center, your heart center expands. The energy moves into an energy "way station" which transports energy up and down the pranic tube, into the chakras and the meridians, as well as expanding and strengthening the aura and other energy structures. Your vibration increases protecting you from lower vibration energies.

Staying in your heart center can also activate and repair natural encodements. The energy from focusing on your heart center can dissolve or de-activate artificial encodements. Such a simple act produces profound changes.

The development of the heart center begins after birth as soon as the infant is placed upon the chest of the mother. When the baby is cradled in loving arms, the energy from the heart center of the mother or other adult pours out to the heart center of the infant. This loving energy gently opens the heart of the infant. The opening of the heart is one of the results of breast feeding. If it is not possible to breast feed, always hold and cuddle the infant. Whenever feeding the infant, whether by bottle or breast, focus on the infant with all the love you have. The infant is receiving crucial nourishment from milk and from the energy of the heart center of the person having the pleasure of feeding the infant.

Whenever you hold the infant, especially the first six months, spend time holding the baby heart-to-heart. Both mother and father need to hold the infant heart-to-heart. If the infant is in a home where there is only one gender, be sure that a loving individual of the other gender spends time holding the infant heart-to-heart. The heart energies of the male and female activate necessary encodements and energies in the infant relating to his/her masculine and feminine aspects.

An additional note: When feeding the infant, be aware of what is happening around you. The energy of an infant is fragile. Think of an infant's energy like translucent butterfly wings. If a butterfly were to land upon you, would you not be gentle? When holding the infant, your energy is enfolding and protecting the energy of the baby. If you are listening to, watching or engaging in conversation or thought contrary to peace, the baby's energy field will be adversely affected. Anyone who has fed an infant is well aware of the baby's reaction to discordant energies.

Staying in your heart also strengthens your physical heart. Just as the heart energy is distributed throughout the rest of the energy system, the heart energy goes directly to the physical heart. There is an energy structure just above and at the top of the physical heart interpenetrating the physical heart. The energy from your heart center goes to this structure and gives strength to the physical heart as well as the cardiovascular system.

You may have read about research studies pertaining to heart health in which it was discovered that diet and supplements were not the primary factors in heart health. The primary factor in heart health is loving and being loved. In other words, the primary exercise, if you will, that will improve your cardiovascular system is exercising your heart center by loving and allowing yourself to be loved!

Begin by focusing on your heart center. Spend time breathing in and out of your heart center. Experiment with focusing on the front of the heart center and then on the back. Then enjoy focusing on both at the same time—a type of bi-location. There are ample opportunities throughout the day to spend even thirty seconds on this exercise. The more time you spend in your heart center, the greater the strength of your physical heart, the greater your intuition, and the stronger your protection from discordant energies surrounding you.

Once you have spent time with the above exercise, experiment focusing on the heart center and each chakra one at a time. Although the heart energy will go to the other chakras through the pranic tube, focusing on your heart and another chakra will deepen the integration of the heart energy with that particular chakra energy.

If you are having difficulties with first chakra issues (family of origin, primary social groups such as religion, culture, race, place of employment), when you focus on the heart center (fourth chakra) and then the first chakra, you will be better able to relate to first chakra issues from a heart-centered perspective.

When your heart focus is also on your second chakra, you will be able to interpret or understand issues of money, sexual relationships, work (separate from the "belonging" aspect of the first chakra), from the broader perspective of the heart energy. That which you wish to create, be it another person or book, music or project, will be infused with the vibration of love.

Heart and third chakra focus will enable you to come to a true love of yourself as you are, not as you wish you could be. When you love yourself as you are, you are better able to move to where you wish to be.

Focusing on both the heart and throat (fifth) center will allow you to express yourself in such a manner that your communication will be more direct and infused with love. That doesn't assure the other person will accept your words, but the vibration of your words will be higher.

The combination of the heart and third eye (sixth chakra) will improve the quality of your thoughts as well as your ability to manifest your plans.

Of course, the combination of heart and crown (seventh) continually strengthens your spiritual connection.

Once you are adept at focusing on two chakras, do three. Imagine the difference in the quality of your thoughts about your childhood if you focused on the sixth, fourth and first. What do you think would happen to your sexual experiences if you focused on your fourth, second and seventh?

The more you understand and work with your energy system, be it chakras, meridians or encodements, the more you discover about your life. As you use the exercises in this and other writings, you will discover your personal power. A victim allows things to happen without taking any action. When you are in your power, you will develop certain patterns of being which strengthen your energy field and allow you to make choices and decisions for your highest good.

Will these exercises give you only a smooth and easy life? No, Dear Ones, but they will assist you in learning how to navigate the ups and downs of life. The only time you will not have ups and downs is when you leave this life.

Discover how much power you have with the above simple exercises.

Next, I will take you through various ways of working with your encodements. Remember, you can have all the information of the universe, but if you do not use it, the power will not be yours.

Accessing Your Power through Encodements

Dear Ones, please read this information from your Heart Source.

The Heart Source

You form the Heart Source through the following steps:

1. Enter into the back of your heart center.
2. Enter into the front of your heart center.
3. Enter into the front of your brow center.
4. Enter into the back of your brow center.
5. Connect your heart center with your brow center with a beam of light moving through your pranic tube from the heart center to the brow.
6. Move that beam of light up to the Center of the Universe (don't worry where that is).
7. Move the light to the center of the earth.

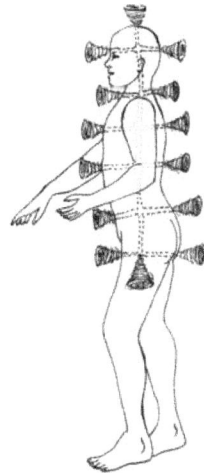

When you drive an automobile, knowing the basic parts of the vehicle and what is needed for their optimum functioning will assist in the car working its best. When you pay attention to the tires, the pressure needed in the tires, the changing of the oil and other maintenance work, you are utilizing all the power of the automobile. If you never pay attention to these necessary details, the car will not perform well.

When you are aware of basic elements needed for your physical body—water, food, rest, movement—then you can learn what will assist your body in functioning to its optimum. When you learn and then actually do that which will assist, then you are harnessing the energy of your body. You do not need to know the body to the same depth as a health care practitioner. You simply need to know and do a few rudimentary actions to access the power in your body.

The same is true for your energy body. You do not need to know the details of the energy anatomy to tap into the power contained within the energy. You simply need to do a few basic activities, most of which revolve around being aware and mindful of your thoughts, actions and feelings.

When you are balanced in body (physical and energy bodies), mind and spirit, you will discover you have the drive, desire and enthusiasm to live life with fullness and joy. Being in balance is the key to living this human life in joy.

It is important to know that the last paragraph is, in fact, a generalization. Each of you came into this incarnation with a particular life plan. Part of that experience revolves around your physical body. You struggle with your physical body in some way. Some of you have tremendous challenges that began with what is called birth defects. Others acquire severe illnesses. Still others cope with certain aches and pains. Even those of you who are in excellent health, but work at keeping your physical body where you would like it, are challenged by your body. And, of course, the major challenge is what you call aging.

Before I lead you through a simple process to work with your encodements, I want to tell you about the importance of your life path. Many of you have asked in great anguish, "What is my purpose? Why am I here? Why can't I discover my purpose? Please tell me my purpose so I can be doing it." Dear Ones, there is no way you cannot be on your path or "doing" your purpose.

We have talked about your Soul Self. As a reminder, know that your Soul Self is who you truly are. Your Soul Self, the fullness of who you are, decided what this aspect of itself, which is your incarnated self, would do, experience and re-member. Your Soul Self knows your mission and purpose. Not only does your Soul Self know your life path, your Soul Self is in control of what happens in your life so that you (the incarnated aspect of yourself) experience exactly what was planned before incarnation. You are on your life path no matter what it is you are doing. Your Soul Self is directing the details of your life. Your choices will make your experiences easier or more difficult…and that part is also planned.

It is important you understand that your Soul Self knows what it is doing. Do you recall the saying, "Let go and let God"? You may not believe that, but it is true. Your Soul Self directed you to read this, all of it or just a part. Remember that your Soul Self makes sure you experience exactly what is according to your plan or even a change in plans.

Do you have free will? Yes…and no. There is a life plan directed by your Soul Self. You, as the persona, have some latitude in how you experience this life plan. For instance, if you planned to experience an illness, you do so more easily if you accept what has happened and follow what you feel motivated to do. You may also choose to be angry at the illness and miss the messages whispered to you from your inner knowing.

Let us now turn to encodements and the opportunity to work with them regarding your physical body. If you read this and do not do the encodement process, know that your Soul Self has directed that. If you say to yourself, "This whole concept of my Soul Self directing me seems like I'm just a puppet. I'm going to prove otherwise," your Soul Self has directed that. If your life plan includes coming into the infinite power that you truly are, your Soul Self will assure this happens. You are an aspect of your Soul Self engaging in this human life with many others also directed by their Soul Selves. If you need some time to process feelings about this, please take time to do so. To do the encodement work, it is not necessary for you to believe any of what was just said about your Soul Self.

Here is how to work with encodements regarding your physical body. Please choose a concern you have about your physical body. It could be weight, aches and pains, an illness, or whatever comes to mind. I will use vision as an example. Please substitute whatever it is that you are addressing.

Step 1: Be in your Heart Source.

Step 2: Go into your heart center from the back. Enter your sacred space and move to your altar deep within the back your heart center.

Step 3: Call the encodement technicians.

Step 4: Ask if there are any artificial encodements affecting your vision. If the answer is "yes," ask what would be the result if you had these removed or de-activated. (See below for discussion on removal or de-activation.) Once you receive the information, you then decide whether or not you accept the consequences. If you accept the consequences, ask the encodement technicians to remove or de-activate the artificial encodements. If you do not want the consequences, simply say "No, thank you."

Step 5: Ask if there are any natural encodements related to your vision that have been damaged or altered. (See below for discussion on damaged or altered.) If the answer is "yes," ask what the consequences would be if you had these repaired. If you accept the consequences, ask that the natural encodements be repaired. If you would rather not have the consequences, simply say "No, thank you."

Step 6: Ask if there are any generational encodements affecting your vision. If the answer is "yes," ask about the consequences. Have the generational encodements de-activated or removed if the consequences are acceptable. Tell them, "No, thank you" if you would rather not have the consequences.

When you first begin doing encodement work, it is important for you to understand the consequences of your request. Any belief, any action, any thought, has consequences. The energy of beliefs, thoughts and actions affects you and others. When you ask that something be done, you are responsible for the consequences. There are often unintended consequences to various actions.

For instance, if you decide to make the way "easier" for another by doing something they should be doing, one unintended consequence could be the individual you assisted did not learn a particular skill or life lesson. When an event occurs in which the individual would need that skill or knowledge s/he was to learn, that person may have a more difficult time. The individual who allowed you to assist him or her also has responsibility in that s/he chose not to learn.

Regarding encodements, what can appear to be a simple change may in fact be a major one. Any request for a change will affect all levels of you. A simple change in vision will not only affect the physical, but will also result in changes on the emotional, mental and spiritual levels. Any change in these areas affects your energy bodies associated with the various levels.

You may ask, for instance, for a change in encodements that will allow you to see without the assistance of corrective lenses. Since the encodements will affect all of your bodies, you may then be able to see more clearly into the hearts of others. When you see more clearly in that way, you may discover something you do not like. You could then decide to end a relationship.

Once encodements are changed, they can be reversed; however, the consequences cannot be reversed. If there were what you judged to be a negative, unintended consequence, those cannot be reversed. But the encodements that resulted in that change can be reversed.

An analogy might be of assistance here. If you change the wiring in your house to assist in one area, the unintended consequence might be that another area would be overloaded. The unintended consequence could result simply in a short in a particular area that is easily corrected, or might result in a fire that is not easily corrected.

I give you this information not to generate fear, but to make you aware of what can occur. Everyone knows that drinking alcohol while driving can have consequences. Most people have no greater consequence than a hangover. Others have consequences that result in physical maiming, jail or death. Once the consequence has occurred, it cannot be changed. You may change the action, drinking in this case, which resulted in the consequence.

Knowing about encodements and how to change them is powerful knowledge. You have access to facilitate change you did not have before. Use this power with wisdom and clarity. Asking the encodement technicians and your Soul Self for additional information will assist you in making wiser decisions.

One individual was inquiring about encodements interfering with a relationship. When she asked about consequences of removing the particular encodements, she discovered that the relationship would indeed be easier in this lifetime. Upon further inquiry, she discovered there would be a change that would result in the next lifetime being more difficult. In her wisdom, she decided to keep things as they were. It was difficult now and she did not want something more difficult later.

The information she received was in alignment with her plan as directed by her Soul Self. In truth, there are no other lifetimes. You play the lead role in many different movies. In this movie, she played the part in which she received information that told her the next lifetime, the next role, would be more difficult if she made these changes.

Know that your Soul Self is in charge of directing this "play" you are in. You cannot make a decision that will thwart your Soul Self. You cannot manipulate your Soul Self. Your Soul Self knows the "big picture." The "big picture" is not just what you view as this particular incarnation. Your "life" has hundreds of parts you play.

If working with encodements were not part of your life path, you would not have been guided to this information. You would not have noticed it or thought it ridiculous. Since you have read this far, know there is something here for you.

There are encodements for every aspect of your life, not just for your physical body. Use the above format to work with encodements regarding emotional health, relationships, abundance, profession, and anything you can think of.

One woman asked for encodements to assist her in driving in another country where the flow of traffic was opposite to what she was accustomed. She asked for a temporary change and driving was much easier. You can work with encodements to assist you in visiting or living in another culture.

Let me give you an example of using encodements regarding work relationships.

If you are having difficulty with someone, ask if there are any artificial encodements interfering with your relationship with the other. Ask about consequences before asking for their removal. Then ask if any natural encodements have been damaged or altered. Ask about consequences before asking for their repair.

Ask if there are any natural encodements with origins in other lifetimes that are interfering with this relationship. (Again, all within the storyline you created for this lifetime.) With these encodements, you want to ask if the reason the encodements were originally placed within you has been fulfilled. If the purpose has not been fulfilled, you need to ask if there is another way to accomplish the purpose of those particular encodements. Again, ask for consequences before having them removed. If it is not appropriate to remove or de-activate natural encodements interfering with the relationship, ask if the technicians could "work around" the encodements in such a way as to facilitate what you desire regarding that relationship. Your encodement work in relationship cannot force someone else to do something contrary to his or her will, path or storyline.

Keep in mind that almost all natural encodements were placed within you by the encodement technicians before your incarnation. Each natural encodement so placed had a specific purpose of furthering why you incarnated upon the Earth plane. When a natural encodement is not damaged or altered, and you wish to remove or change it, the ultimate decision for this rests with the infinite aspect of yourself, which you know is your Soul Self. You may ask for the encodements to be removed due to the discomfort you are feeling, but your Soul Self, your infinite aspect, the *You* who knows the "big picture," can overrule you. The only time that will happen is if you will be diverted from what it is you came here to experience.

In this movie you are playing, your Soul Self always has your best interests at heart, even if it does not seem so. One major way to access your power is to trust your Soul Self. You do this by allowing what is, to be. When you fight against what is, you use your precious energy to fight unwinnable battles. Use your energy for living in the now, not for fighting against what is. Most problems in life result from trying to force your will to change what happened in the past or to fit your view of the future.

Changes can be made. The large majority of these changes will be made in the area of removing artificial encodements and repairing damaged natural encodements. When you wish to change a natural encodement, ask your Soul Self if this is in alignment with your movie. If your Soul Self says you need to experience this particular encodement, ask if there is another way without having to...(fill in the blank).

There are times natural encodements can remain active when no longer needed. This is especially true in the areas of grief and life changes such as profession or moving to a different location.

Let me discuss grief first.

The primary reason encodements regarding relationship remain open after the ending of the relationship is due to the reluctance, even refusal, to let go. I mentioned earlier that the major source of pain in life is the refusal of what is. Someone leaving through death or other means (divorce, estrangement) has the greatest effect upon the remaining person. You are a communal being. The primary mode of experience in this life is through relationship. Here you learn about the power of love, what love is and isn't, control, acceptance, letting go, setting boundaries, and much more.

When someone dies and you were bonded to him/her in either a positive or negative manner, you have natural and artificial encodements relating to that relationship. The natural encodements were placed there before your incarnation. The artificial encodements were built around and upon the natural encodements during the course of your relationship. When you stay in grief and longing for one who has left, you may choose to change the encodements surrounding the relationship. Ask that any natural encodements regarding the relationship be removed or de-activated.

Removing or de-activating these encodements does not remove the person or experience from your life. It does not totally remove the grief but will lessen the grief. This process will allow you to release the individual more easily. Your encodements regarding the death of someone in your life have a built-in deactivation pattern according to your particular culture. Life experience with this individual could have damaged the encodements or formed artificial encodements which kept active the natural encodements beyond their original intention.

When you ask that these encodements be removed or de-activated, you are, in fact, accepting what is. The active role of the individual in your life is now finished. All that was set into motion by that one is now accomplished. The ripples of that person in your life will continue to expand in ways you, on the conscious level, are unaware.

How does this happen? Not all encodements are active when you incarnate. Encodements are activated at certain developmental stages. Someone else's purpose in your life may be to activate or strengthen certain encodements, e.g., you may have no desire to have children until you love someone so much that you wish to have a child with him or her. Your encodements to have children were activated by the love in that relationship.

In addition, artificial encodements are developed through relationship. You might form many artificial encodements during the course of life with someone. When that person is gone, these encodements are still in place. This is how the ripples of one's presence in your life continue. You can request that these encodements be changed, de-activated or removed. When this is in alignment with the reason you incarnated, your Soul Self will facilitate the process at your request.

Doing encodement work is an example of what you in the Christian tradition heard from the one you call Jesus, "Ask and it will be done." Because you are aware of the encodement structure, you are requesting that structure to be aligned according to your desire. When you pray, "Please release me from the pain of losing my partner," you are making a request that, when accomplished, will have changed your encodements. Encodement work has the same result but you are aware of how it happens.

You, in conjunction with your Soul Self, have the power to set your direction. If there is in your movie the experience of learning a lesson, and you don't know how to learn it, ask. Your Soul Self is willing to assist. If, in your life plan, it is a lesson you thought you had learned, ask if there is additional learning to acquire. There are varying degrees of the illusion of learning in every life plan. For some things you might need to experience and learn on a superficial level. For others you may need to experience on a deeper level. Every person is different. When you attempt to gauge yourself by someone else, you will be off the mark. You are the only gauge of yourself.

Remember, this is all in the context of your movie. As an infinite being you have nothing to learn.

If you do not believe you can "hear" what is being said to you by spiritual helpers, then simply accept what is happening. Your Soul

Self is adept at placing before you exactly what you need. Accept what is, not in the sense of the passivity of giving up, but in the sense of calm watchfulness. When you accept what is, you will be better able to note the messages your Soul Self is sending to you through other people and even such things as billboards, music and other media.

When you are angry, fearful or despondent, you remain in a position of victim, which is a negation of your personal power. When you ask "Why?" with no intention of listening, you will remain in victim mode. If you ask "Why?" with the desire to hear what you want to hear but are not open to the true answer, you remain in victim mode. It may not be for you to know "Why."

However, if you ask, "What now? What is needed for me to move on?" and listen with your heart, moving in accordance with your heart, then you are in your power. There is tremendous power in listening. There is little power in flailing at the universe. Flailing only disperses energy and weakens you. Use the tools you have. Most of you have numerous tools that would assist you, but you "forget" to use them or choose not to use them. When you use what is available to you, you are accessing your power.

Let's further examine accessing power by using encodements in another area of your life. For this example, I will use changing your profession. You may choose another area if you wish. Simply follow the format.

The first step is to ask yourself, "Am I happy doing what I do now? Do I feel fulfilled in my current line of work? Have I ever felt happy and fulfilled in my current job?" The answers to these questions will let you know if you ever did find the profession you were best suited. If the answers to the above are, "No," you then follow or adapt this particular format for working with your encodements. (This is a general format. Use your own inner knowing, which is accessing your personal power, to know what questions to ask.)

After connecting with your encodement technicians, ask the following questions:

"Do I have natural encodements for the work I am presently doing?"

1. If the answer is "No, you don't have the encodements" then no wonder you are having a difficult time. See below to find the encodements for what you would be best suited.

2. If the answer is "Yes, you have the encodements," ask, "Are they damaged or altered in such a way that has resulted in my not feeling fulfilled?" If the answer is "Yes, they are damaged or altered," then you can ask the consequences of their being repaired. If the consequences are agreeable to you, have them repaired. (If you do not want them repaired because the consequence would be that you would enjoy your present line of work and you'd rather change positions, please have them repaired anyway. You can then follow the procedure below for changing profession.)

3. If the answer is "Yes, you have the encodements and they are not damaged," ask if they are fully activated. Activate them, if need be. (Again, if you wish to change professions, please do activate and continue the process outlined below.)

4. If the answer is "Yes, you have the encodements" and they are not damaged and they are fully activated, ask, "Has the purpose for these encodements been fulfilled?" If "No," ask what needs to be done to fulfill their purpose. You may also ask if it is necessary to have the purpose fulfilled.

5. Next, ask, "Are there any artificial encodements interfering with my being fulfilled in my present position?" If the answer is "Yes," please ask about con-sequences of repairing or de-activating these encode-ments. Let your inner knowing guide your choice. This

is how you exercise your personal power. (Again, if the only reason not to repair them is because you would enjoy your position and you'd like to leave, please have them repaired and follow the procedure below.)

You will continue with natural encodements already in place. Ask the encodement technicians to show you encodements present for profession. They will "light up" in some way. Now ask, "What professions do these encodements hold?" Are the encodements active, inactive, damaged or altered? If damaged or altered, have them repaired.

If you are unsatisfied with your current position, but do not know what you would like to do next, the above information will give you a direction. Once you establish a direction, the process continues below.

Do you know what it is you would like to do? If so, are there already encodements for that position? If there are, be sure no artificial encodements are interfering. Next, ascertain whether all natural encodements for that area are in good condition and are active.

Following are the steps to implant encodements for a profession or job where you have not detected natural encodements previously placed within you. (Remember, your Soul Self is directing everything. Relax and let go.)

1. As clearly and in as much detail as possible, define what it is you wish to do. Spend time having fun imagining as much as possible what you would like. Pay attention to your feelings. Does this "feel" right to you? Draw some pictures, sing a song, dance it, map it. Use whatever tools will assist you in fully accessing what you would like to do.

2. Connect with your Soul Self. If you do not have your own method for doing this, you may go into your heart center from the back, go deep into your sacred space or altar, and ask to speak to your Soul Self. Ask

your Soul Self to show you at least three possibilities of what this position would look like for you. Get as clear a picture as possible from one scene before you move onto another. You may want to take time to write down or tape your reflections before moving to your next scene. You may ask for more than three possibilities if you wish.

3. After you have fully engaged with a possibility, ask to be shown what happened that resulted in that particular possibility. Did you need to learn something, was there a feeling or attitude that persisted or changed, etc.?

4. Was there any possibility you did not want? Was there a possibility you did like? Were there two or more possibilities in which you liked some aspects but not others? Consult with your Soul Self regarding any questions you may have. Remember, your Soul Self is the one who knows the "Master Plan" for your life. Your Soul Self is the aspect of yourself that is infinite, limitless and omniscient. Your Soul Self will be sure your new profession or job is in alignment with what you wished to experience in this lifetime.

5. When you are ready to make the change, ask that the encodements relating to your present position and not needed for your next endeavor, be de-activated. Be sure all artificial encodements acquired through the past position are de-activated or removed. In addition, ask that any artificial encodements that would potentially interfere with your new profession be removed or de-activated. Only do this after you are ready to step into the energy of your new position.

6. Ask the encodement technicians to align your encodement system to your new profession. They will put in the necessary natural encodements, adjust others that are current, and de-activate any others that would interfere.

I give you three small pieces of further information.

Some may have questions as to the phrase "remove or de-activate." The earlier in life artificial encodements are acquired, the greater the number of additional artificial encodements built around them forming a separate energy structure known as a thought form. The encodement technicians know the best way to work with the encodements. They will know whether to fully remove the energy or simply make it non-functional.

With reference to your heart center, the more you stay in the energy of your heart, your higher vibrational energy will naturally and with ease dissolve or de-activate artificial encodements. In fact, staying in your heart center can change entire artificial encodement structures that were begun before birth. This is especially true if you stay in your Heart Source. Natural encodements that were damaged or altered can also be repaired.

The last piece of information is to remind you that, as a nightly practice, it is beneficial to ask that all artificial encodements developed that day be removed. (They will have few, if any, additional encodements built upon them.) You will also find it helpful to ask for the repair of any damaged or altered natural encodements that occurred that day.

And, finally, Dear Ones, remember that you were made from Love. That means that you are Love. You are Love Incarnate. You are also dearly beloved.

Using the Power of Your Heart

Dear Ones, Please read this information while in your Heart Source.

The Heart Source

You form the Heart Source through the following steps:

1. Enter into the back of your heart center.
2. Enter into the front of your heart center.
3. Enter into the front of your brow center.
4. Enter into the back of your brow center.
5. Connect your heart center with your brow center with a beam of light moving through your pranic tube from the heart center to the brow.
6. Move that beam of light up to the Center of the Universe (don't worry where that is).
7. Move the light to the center of the earth.

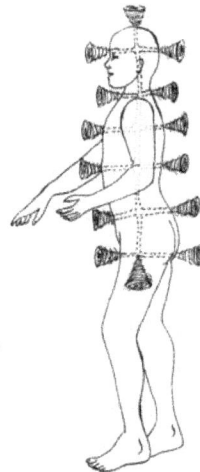

I have given a brief outline of your energy system, the encodement system and how to contact the encodement technicians.

I have also discussed the importance of the heart center and Heart Source. We will now focus on the power of the heart. Please do not pass over this information thinking you know all there is to know about your heart and heart center. Few people are aware of this information, although all of you have access to this knowledge. Having this knowledge and *using it* will assist you in activating the power you have within you to make positive changes in your life. As you have heard, knowledge is power. However, this is only true if you use this knowledge. Use what is here and you will be amazed at what can happen.

The nature of communication requires that I discuss the two aspects of the heart in a linear manner. By this I mean that I am not able to relate the information in such a way that you immediately "see" the interconnection of the heart and heart center. Although I will speak of them as two separate aspects of yourself, they are one and work as one. What happens to one results in changes to the other. Their relationship with each other is synergistic. Another way of saying this is that the effect they have in relationship with each other is 1 + 1 is much greater than 2. Whatever you do to increase the efficiency of your heart center or your physical heart will produce an energetic reaction that is exponential in its effect.

As you well know, there is your physical heart and your heart center, often called heart chakra. Your heart chakra is the entryway into your energy system. When you enter your heart center from the front, the way most people are taught, you enter into the dimension of this incarnation. You are able to move throughout your energy system when you enter from the front. From this space, you are able to examine your own energy system, find blockages or congestion, and make repairs.

Let me take you through a few exercises. Once you have experienced these simple techniques, you can expand upon them and go where you feel motivated. If an idea comes to you on how to use this information in a different manner, please implement your idea. Set your intention to connect with me and I will guide you!

Cathy Chapman

Have paper and pencil or pen. If you have a recorder, that might be easier as you will be able to talk into the recorder as you are making your discoveries.

Remember, although I am speaking of the heart chakra and the energy structure in the physical heart as if they are separate, they are interrelated.

Move first into your heart chakra from the front. For those needing assistance in this, simply focus your attention on your heart chakra. It is in the center of your chest just to the right of your physical heart. (The physical heart is generally located just to the left of the midline of the body. Some have their physical heart further to the right than the general population. If you are one of these, just know that the heart center is in the center of the chest area.) Feel your consciousness entering into the heart chakra. You can also imagine being a few inches tall and walking into the heart chakra.

Imagine breathing in and out of this center. If this is a new experience for you, give yourself a few minutes. When you are in this area, you will find your mind calming down. Simply breathe in and out. Close your eyes if this is helpful for you. Continue breathing in and out.

Know that you do not have to "work" at following the instructions. Your intention will establish what will happen. Simply allow. If your thoughts or your left-brain interfere, tell it everything is fine and be at peace. Then go back to these instructions. Being able to calm your mind by focusing on the heart center and breathing in and out of the heart center is another way of exercising your personal power.

Some people ask, "How do I know I'm where you want me to be?" I will ask you to move your awareness or consciousness from place to place in your energy field. If you are concerned you cannot do this, try the following. Without looking at your leg, bring your awareness to your right hip. Notice the feel of your clothes on your hip. Notice if there is any pressure or sensation at your hip. Now, without looking at the hip, imagine moving down the outside of your leg. Note how each part of your leg feels. Notice how clothes or the air feels upon your leg. Now move your awareness along the outside of your foot to the big toe. Again, notice any pressure. You will do the same with your energy field, even if you are not aware of how it is structured. Trust your inner knowing which is all knowing.

You are now going on a tour of your energy field. I will not take you through every structure as there are many. I will take you through basic structures. You can then use this process, or adapt it as needed, to assess other energy structures.

This is where you might find a tape recorder or pencil and paper handy. Write or speak the first thing that comes to your mind. Some of you may describe impressions in a literal manner. Others will use symbolic language. If what comes to you seems strange, don't worry. Record it and examine it later for symbolic representation. Later you can meditate on the symbol and discover its meaning for you.

Since we have addressed the chakra system, we will begin there. If you are not that familiar with the chakras, refer to the diagram on page 57. Let us begin.

You are in your heart center. Set your intention to move to the first chakra, which is at the base of your spine. In a sense, you are in two places at once—your heart center and your first chakra. The color of the first chakra is red. It should be spinning in a clockwise direction as if you were looking up at it from below. (Note: If you are in the southern hemisphere, it will spin in a counter or anti-clockwise direction.) Ask yourself the following questions and take the first thought or impression that comes to you. Even if you believe it was your own thought, write it down or record it.

1. What color is the chakra? Is there more than one color present? What do these colors mean?

2. Is there any congestion or sluggishness in that chakra?

3. Is it spinning clockwise? Is it spinning fully? Is it blocked in any manner?

4. Is there something in the chakra that does not belong there? There could be thought forms (anger, fear, sadness, shame, etc.) or other energies present. If something else is present, ask what it is.

5. Is there any damage to the chakra? Is the "screen" over the chakra strong and complete? Are the "petals" of the chakra in good shape? Are any petals torn or bent out of position?

6. What is the main issue causing problems with this chakra?

Now move up to the second chakra. Be sure you are still in your heart center. The second chakra is an inch or two below your navel. Chakras two through six have both a front and a back. The second chakra is orange. Both the front and back spin clockwise if you are looking at the chakra from the front or back. Just know this and don't allow your left-brain to be tied in knots trying to figure out how it looks or works.

Now ask:

1. What color is the chakra? Is there more than one color present? What do these colors mean?

2. Is there any congestion in that chakra?

3. Are the front and back aspects of the chakra in balance?

4. Are both the front and back spinning clockwise? Spinning fully? Is the chakra blocked in any manner?

5. Is there something in the chakra that does not belong there? There could be thought forms (anger, fear,

sadness, shame, etc.) or other energies present. If something else is present, ask what it is.

6. Is there any damage to the chakra? Is the "screen" over the chakra strong and complete? Are the "petals" of the chakra in good shape? Are any torn or out of position?

7. What is the main issue causing problems with this chakra?

Now, move up to the third chakra. It is in the solar plexus area just below your sternum. Again, this chakra is in both the front and the back. This chakra is yellow. Ask the same questions you asked for the second chakra.

Move up to the fourth chakra, both front and back. This is your heart center where we began this exercise. The color for this chakra is green. Ask the same questions you asked for the second chakra.

Continue by moving up to the throat center. This fifth chakra is in the hollow at the base of your neck. This one is blue. Again, ask the same questions you asked for the second chakra.

The sixth is the brow chakra. It is in the middle of your forehead just above the brow. The back is at the bony ridge about an inch or so above the bottom of your skull. This chakra is indigo in color. Some see it as a deep purple. Answer the same questions as before for this chakra.

The last chakra is the crown, which is at the top of the head where the soft spot was when you were a baby. Some people see this chakra as violet. Others see it as golden and still others see it as sparkling white light. This chakra is only at the crown. There is no front and back. Use the questions listed for the first chakra for this seventh chakra.

You have a wealth of information simply from this exercise. If you are tired, please take a break before you continue the rest of the exercise. The assessment or evaluation I am giving you can be done in stages. You may be led to do only certain parts of this process. If you follow the entire process, you will have a fairly complete assessment of your major energy structures. With the information you are gathering, you will be able to facilitate your own healing.

There is a structure many call the pranic tube. This channel runs from above your crown, in through your crown, through your spine, straight down into the Earth. It is a tube of energy. The tube is an energy structure on a different dimension than the physical, although it is within the physical.

Check to be sure you are in your heart center. Set your intention to move into your pranic tube. This might feel like moving toward the back of your heart center into the spine. Make a note if you had any difficulty moving into the pranic tube. Was there any sense of a blockage? The pranic tube, as well as its pathway into each chakra, can become congested. Move upward until you are about eighteen inches above your head.

Now move down the pranic tube evaluating its "health." You may find congestion or damage anywhere along the tube itself, or in the connection between the pranic tube and the chakras. Again, write or record your impressions. Take the first thought that comes to you. Allow the impressions to come. There is no need to force them. Attempting to force impressions activates the left-brain and often has you doubting what you receive.

Begin to move your awareness gently down the pranic tube. Note the following:

1. Does it seem easy or difficult to move up and down the tube?

2. Does the pranic tube seem to be straight and even?

3. Do you "feel" anything present that does not seem to be there? Simply ask, "Does this belong?" and take the "yes" or "no" that you receive.

You will do an evaluation of the connection of the pranic tube with each chakra. The crown (seventh) and root (first) chakras each have a vertical entryway or access point into the pranic tube. The other chakras have horizontal connections to the pranic tube going from the front of the chakra to the pranic and from the back of the chakra to the pranic tube. They do not "meet" at the pranic tube because they are in different dimensions.

When doing this assessment, move your awareness or consciousness into the chakra from the pranic tube and, in chakras two through six, horizontally to the front of the chakra and to the back. The clearer the pranic tube and its connection to each chakra, the more easily the energy moves up and down the tube, between the chakras and the pranic tube, and from chakra to chakra.

As you come to the chakras, ask:

1. Does the pathway from the pranic tube to the front of the chakra appear clear? Does the pathway from the pranic tube to the back of the chakra appear clear? Is it easy to move from the pranic tube into the chakra?

2. Does the pathway appear straight and even?

3. Do you find anything in the pathway between the pranic tube and front and the back of the chakra that does not appear to belong?

4. For chakras two through six, move your awareness from the pranic tube forward to the chakra. Does that pathway appear straight and even? Any congestion? Anything there that doesn't belong?

You have now assessed the health of each chakra, the pranic tube, and the pathway of the pranic tube to each chakra. You have gleaned valuable information. You may continue with the assessment of your energy field or go below to the section on how to use your heart center to bring healing to any irregularities you have found. Some people want all the information at one time. Others feel overwhelmed by too much information and prefer to gather some information and then do the healing. It does not matter. You can choose to work with the healing of just one chakra or energy "part" at a time if you wish. Follow your inner knowing.

Another part of your energy center is your hara line. This line runs roughly in the middle of your body in front of the spine. This line is not on the physical level but affects the physical level. If your hara line is not strong, if it is broken or bent, you will have a number of physical complaints. Your hara line contains the energy of your incarnation. It holds your physical body in place.

To assess the health of your hara line, simply go into the center of your heart from the front. If you prefer, you can also access this energy from the back of the heart center. When deeply within your heart center, set your intention to move your awareness to your hara line. Just trust you are there.

You will now assess your hara line in stages:

1. From eighteen inches above your head to your crown chakra.

2. From the crown chakra to an area about two inches below your throat chakra (known as the soul star by some).

3. From the soul contact to a couple of inches above the navel (core star).

4. From the core star to the tan tien (about 2 or 2.5 inches below the navel).

5. From the tan tien to the earth star about eighteen inches below the earth.

Move to the point about eighteen inches above your head. For ease, I'm calling this the origination point. This is where it enters your energy field forming your identification point for this lifetime.

Now ask the following questions taking the first answer that pops into your head.

1. What is the quality of the origination point of my hara line? Is it strong?

2. Is there anything interfering with the hara line at this point?

3. Does it appear bent or broken at this point?

4. Does the hara line continue from this point and move in a straight line downward?

Follow your hara line from this point downward to a few inches below your throat chakra. There is an energy structure there. People call it various names. For my purposes, I will call it the soul contact. If you have another name for this area, please use it. For the assessment, set your intention to move to the soul contact through the hara line. The purpose is to move down the hara line and notice what is there.

As you move down the hara line to the soul contact, ask the following questions:

1. Do I move easily down my hara line from above my head to the soul contact?

2. Is the path of my hara line straight and smooth? Are there any bends or breaks? If so, where and in what direction?

3. Is the hara line the same width from one point to the next?

4. Does the energy of the hara line appear strong and healthy?

5. Is there any congestion in the hara line?

6. Does the hara line move fully into the soul contact point?

7. Is the soul contact center clear and healthy?

The next section of the hara line to assess is from the soul contact to the core star, about two or three inches above the navel within the energy body, aligned with the hara line. Ask the above questions substituting the words "core star" for "soul star."

The next section of the hara line runs from the core star to the tan tien. The tan tien is on the same energy level as the hara line and is about 2 or 2.5 inches below the navel. Use the same questions as above substituting the words "tan tien."

The last section you will assess is from the hara line to the earth star which is twelve to eighteen inches below the Earth depending upon the individual. Again, use the questions above substituting the appropriate words.

Now that you have assessed the haric level, you may either continue your energy body assessment or move to the sections below on healing.

The above gives you a blueprint on how to assess various energy structures. You may use the same process for assessing the aura, the meridians, acupuncture points and any other energy structure. You may make your assessment as broad or as detailed as you wish. Trust yourself. Trust your inner knowing. Do what "feels" right to you.

Let me make a detour here. I have said several times to trust yourself, trust your inner knowing. I realize that many of you are reluctant to do so because you have found yourself in difficult situations when you have previously trusted yourself. One of the biggest difficulties is separating what you believe your inner knowing is "telling" you from what your human self wants to do.

There are several methods of contacting your inner knowing to eliminate or lessen the influence of your human wants and desires (some call this the ego or negative ego). When fully within your Heart Source you are better able to discern between what comes from your mind or little ego and what is from your Soul Self.

If you are not comfortable with the Heart Source, go deeply into your heart center. You may do this from the front or the back. Be sure you are deep within your heart center. Breathe in and out of your heart to assist you in centering more completely in your heart. Experiment with entering into the front and then the back of your heart center. Find which works best for you. You will know you are deep within your heart center when thoughts slow down or even cease. Ask questions from this space. Answers from deep within the heart center are usually reliable.

Another way to increase your confidence in your inner knowing is to work with someone you trust. The two of you can do these exercises together. Compare notes. Receiving similar results is affirming and boosts your self-confidence. The more confident you are, the more you will trust your inner knowing and the more powerful you will become. When this occurs, you will begin receiving more information. This happens because your trust opens the pathways for information to come to you. The information is always there. What you receive depends upon your own openness and awareness. The more confident, the more open you are, the more personal power you access.

Healing Your Chakras

You are now going to use the information you gained from the assessment and focus on your heart center to facilitate healing. Let's say you have some congestion in your throat or fifth chakra.

For this experience, be deep within your Heart Source. Now move into your heart center from the front. (If you are not yet comfortable with the Heart Source, you may simply focus on the heart center.) While holding an awareness of the space deep within your heart center, focus on your throat chakra. Set your intention that your throat center clear. Allow the energy of your heart center in conjunction with your intention and your focus on the throat center to do its work. No need to force anything. Simply set your intention for clearing of the throat center while focusing on your heart center. Hold this connection for at least a minute and allow these powerful energies to work together.

When you set your intention, you are accessing your power for self-healing. The more focused you are, the more easily the energies work together to clear the chakra. Gentle focused intent works best. Simply set your intention, hold your focus, and allow the powerful energies you have set into motion do their work. Hold this focus for as long as you can or until you feel it is complete. Repeat as many times as you feel necessary.

For healing any aspect of your energy system, simply be in your heart center. Bring your focus to the aspect you wish to heal. Set your intention to clear, repair or clear, or any other action which come to you. Witness what happens. Observe and allow. Your focused intention in union with the power of your heart center, especially if you are in your Heart Source, is all you need. Refrain from forcing anything. Just as you allow a wound on your body to heal without "forcing" it, allow the wisdom inherent in your energy field to heal that which you set into motion through your intention.

Remember, you can do this with any part of your energy field. You can work with your aura as a whole or a particular layer or part of your aura. You can focus on the entire meridian system, one meridian, or one acupuncture point. The more specific you are in your intention, the more specific your healing will be.

As you work with this simple technique, your own inner wisdom may give you suggestions of other things you can do to enhance the healing. One is to work with your encodement technicians asking them to remove artificial encodements, repair altered or damaged natural encodements, and activate inactive natural encodements pertaining to the particular damage in your energy field.

If you facilitate healing in others, no matter what technique you use, you will find the energy enhanced by:

1. Begin in your Heart Source.

2. Connecting heart-to-heart with the other.

3. Focusing on the part of the other's energy field you wish to balance.

4. Setting your intention.

5. Continue with your chosen energy modality.

The heart-to-heart connection enhances and amplifies healing. In fact, the heart-to-heart connection is healing in and of itself. If you are with someone in pain, or are concerned about someone, and are having difficulty communicating with him or her, simply "see" energy move from your heart to his or her heart. Again, do not force the connection. Once you form the intention, the connection will occur if the other person allows it. If you are blocked from making the connection, the other person is telling you "No." Honor their request.

Let's examine what you can do from the back of your heart center. (Again, everything is easier and more powerful if you are in your Heart Source.) By entering the back of the heart center, you are able to access energies in other dimensions, universes and times. You can trace or map the history of an issue in your life through lifetimes, connect and communicate with those who have shared other lifetimes with you, and speak to those guides who have journeyed with you on the inner plane in various lifetimes.

We'll work with one example and then you can use it as a model for any other traveling or communication you would like to do. Begin with the process of tracing an issue in your present lifetime through other lifetimes. You will even be able to go into the possibilities of future lifetimes regarding that issue.

Before we begin the actual exercise, I want to share with you some thoughts about living other lifetimes which many of you may not know on a conscious level. (I remind you of what was said earlier about all being an illusion except Love and Oneness.) You, of course, are familiar with the concept of Oneness. You are one with all, all is one with you. I am one with you. You are one with me.

You are experiencing life in a physical form as you have done many times. (Again, all is in the context of this being an illusion, a creation for you to have multiple experiences.) As you live your life, your experiences have an influence on the Oneness just as what happens to the leaf of a tree affects the tree as a whole. There is a resonance within the Oneness with all thoughts, words, actions and events.

When you leave a particular lifetime, the energy of the experiences and knowledge you have gathered are, as it were, deposited into the energy of the Oneness. When you enter into another lifetime, you gather to yourself the energy of experiences from all other lifetimes. You select what you need for your particular lifetime.

You may ask, "Do I not bring with me the experiences of my particular soul for each lifetime?" Dear One, you will understand this in its fullness when you have left this lifetime. There is only Oneness. Before incarnating you (your Soul Self) looked into the prop room and took the attitudes and beliefs, events and happenings you needed to experience what you desired in this particular lifetime. You also brought with you, in this amazing illusion you have created, the illusion of other lifetimes.

"Ah," you may say, "you said 'before I incarnate.' Does that not demonstrate I am a specific soul?" Yes, the words do seem to imply that. Consider, however, that you may be aware of the concept of Oneness and teach others that all is One. How do you then bring about the understanding that you are separate within the Oneness? Analogies such as the vine and the branches, the leaf and tree, as well as others are used. Very few people, however, truly have an experience of what Oneness is. I leave you to ruminate over these words.

When tracing the energy of an issue through lifetimes, you are addressing the energy you collected before incarnating. No matter what your philosophy about past lifetimes, this exercise can be of great benefit to you.

Healing through the Illusion of Lifetimes

Begin by choosing an issue to examine. This could be a relationship with someone in your life, a behavior pattern, a feeling, vocation or work, or anything that interests you. If you wish, you can ask your Soul Self to present to you a subject. Once you are ready, enter your heart center from the back and go deep within to your altar or sacred space. (If possible, be in your Heart Source.) Breathe in and out of your heart center. Ground into the Earth by imagining you are growing roots from your feet and dropping a line of energy from your tailbone into the center of the Earth.

You will activate your journey by setting your intention. Ask to go to the place in your heart center that takes you to other lifetimes. Simply allow your consciousness to go there. Now state, in these or similar words, "I go now to the most recent lifetime which has the greatest effect upon ..." Allow your consciousness to move to that lifetime. You may or may not have images of the particular lifetime. For this experience, it does not matter. (If you wish to receive particular images, I suggest you do a formal past-life regression with a trained practitioner.)

Begin to write or record whatever impressions come to you. Set your intention for healing anything in this past lifetime that has affected your current incarnation. Focusing on your heart center, ask for the healing of all your chakras as it relates to your intention. You may ask for healing of one chakra at a time in the order you choose, or you may simply ask for the healing of all chakras. Do this same process for any aspects of your energy anatomy you choose.

When you are ready, you may then set your intention to move to the next lifetime which has the greatest effect upon the issue you have in mind. Repeat the process. If you have the thought, "I need to rest before doing another," please listen to your inner knowing. This type of energy work takes energy! You are expending energy in your focus. You are expending energy in your healing.

When you have finished whatever travel you wish to do, come back to your heart center. Stand in your sacred space or at your altar. Breathe deeply. Ask the encodement technicians to harmonize your entire encodement system to the vibrations of the energies of healing you have just experienced. Allow energy from the Earth and from above to come into you. Feel this energy coursing through your system. Come out of the back of your heart center and into your physical body. Take a deep breath and honor yourself for the work you have completed.

You may adapt this process to travel to other planets, other dimensions, and to contact other beings. Have fun. The basic elements in this process are being in the sacred space, your altar, by entering the back of your heart center. Anchor yourself by growing roots from your feet and dropping a line of energy from your tailbone down into the center of the earth. Set your intention. Make the request.

There are, of course, other ways to achieve these same ends. I give you this as one possibility. You may be inspired in adapting this process to better suit you personally.

Each time you use one of the exercises that I or another have given you, you develop a skill. You learn. You expand the boundaries of your sense of limitation. These are all ways of discovering and using your power. You might find it easier to use these exercises by joining with others and lead each other through the process.

This message has touched upon what you can do from the back of your heart center. While you are there, ask what else you can do. If you have an idea that comes to you, try it out. Listen to yourself. You are of the Oneness and there is infinite knowledge in the Oneness.

Remember, you are beloved and you are Love Incarnate!

———•———

You and Your Soul Self

Dear Ones, Read this information while in your Heart Source.

The Heart Source

You form the Heart Source through the following steps:

1. Enter into the back of your heart center.
2. Enter into the front of your heart center.
3. Enter into the front of your brow center.
4. Enter into the back of your brow center.
5. Connect your heart center with your brow center with a beam of light moving through your pranic tube from the heart center to the brow.
6. Move that beam of light up to the Center of the Universe (don't worry where that is).
7. Move the light to the center of the earth.

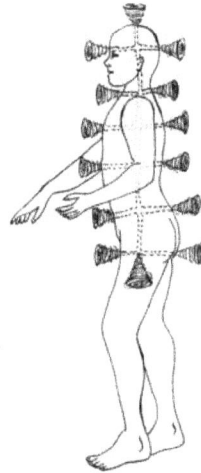

Some are asking how your Soul Self, the Oneness of yourself, interacts with you in your current incarnation. I understand your curiosity about this relationship. I also understand why some are concerned about being a "puppet" since your Soul Self is the one directing you. These thoughts come from a lack of understanding about what your Soul Self and your persona truly are.

First and foremost, there is no separation between you and your Soul Self. You are one. There is no separation between your toes and the rest of your body. Your body is one. The difficulty in understanding the relationship between your Soul Self and your current persona is dualistic thinking. You have difficulty comprehending what it means to be one with your Soul Self. Even the language "one with Soul Self" implies there are two separate beings. There is only one being. That one being is you.

Before incarnation you were in your fullness. You knew, experienced, and reveled in your fullness and the unity of your fullness with the Oneness. You did not need anyone to explain it to you. You lived it and you knew it. There was not any question about duality or being separate. In fact, being separate could be another name for what some call "hell."

I will speak now about how you planned your incarnations. Due to the confines of language, I will need to use terms implying there is "time" and there is "separateness." There is neither. Even though I tell you this, you will not truly understand what I am saying. You do have the intellectual knowledge from your learning, but you do not *know* this until you discover this in the very depths of yourself where there is only the Oneness.

Before there was any concept of time, when you first became aware of yourself as a part of the Oneness, as a wave identified as part of the wholeness of the ocean, you wanted to have various experiences. Others such as yourself began to join together to have these experiences. You began to consult with each other. As you consulted, you also began to specialize. Some of you wanted to experience great public power, others wealth, still others poverty. Some of you became mentors, healers and warriors. It didn't really matter what you experienced.

Cathy Chapman

You created challenges for yourself...the greatest of which was the illusion of "forgetting" your infinity. Groups of you joined together to create the illusion of challenges on the earth plane adding more complexity. As an infinite being you created amazing scenarios all based on the "forgetting" of who you truly are—an infinite being, the power and presence of God. Now, with 6.5 billion human souls on your planet, the complexity is truly great.

Each of you began to develop an overall plan for these experiences. Think of it as an outline to a book. When you plan a book, you develop the theme, each chapter and the plot development. Your life, and by "life" I mean the journey of your soul in the experience of limitation, can be likened to a very large book. Each of your incarnations is a chapter. You meticulously planned each chapter, each lifetime. Others joined you in the planning and in the execution of your grand creation of experiencing limitation. You created what your life would be as well as the roles others were to play in your incarnation. Each of you did this.

Once you decided what you wanted to happen in your incarnation, you worked with the encodement technicians. The encodement technicians set the energy structure for the grand illusion of the life of _____ (insert your name here) by placing within you the encodements attracting you to the experiences you desired.

I'm going to mix metaphors in order to assist you in understanding what happens.

When you make the plans for your incarnation, you develop a blueprint of what you want to happen. Think of this as the blueprint an architect uses to guide the builders of your house. The encodement technicians then enter and put in the "wiring" according to your plans. The encodements attract you to people, places and things, giving you options and opportunities. There are also encodements to "hide" things from you. No one is able to experience everything in life during an incarnation. The various encodements help you "build" the life you planned before incarnating.

Switching to the metaphor of a play, your encodements are activated according to certain cues in your life. Just as an actor knows to come onto stage when a certain line is given, so certain encodements become active with particular events in your life. Developmental encodements are "set" to become active at particular ages or as you attain certain developmental milestones. An active encodement attracts you to an experience in your life. Unless you have an active encodement, there will be no attraction to a particular person, place, lifestyle, and more. There are encodements repelling you from particular persons, places, etc. Some encodements are strong to "neutralize" your attraction to certain people. This occurs when souls with deep relationships on "the other side" are playing a different role in incarnated life.

Continuing the metaphor of the play or movie, you and those in your life take on certain roles. You have heard this many times. Few people realize the depth of this truth. You are "play acting." You take on a role that is not truly you. You do such a wonderful job you would win what you call an Academy Award. Each person in your life would win an Academy Award for his or her role in relationship with you. All of you are Academy Award players or Tony award winners using the play metaphor. Every person who is in your life you created to play a specific role in your play. The person agreed to take that part for you.

How, you may ask, could you have created someone to play a particular role? If an individual plays one role with me, wouldn't they play the same role with everyone else? No, no one plays the same role with every person. An individual may be a villain of a parent to one child and then a beloved saint of a parent for another child. The one known as thief to some may be beloved friend to others. Souls play different roles with different people. That is why some people could go to the same event and some believe the presenter is wonderful and others abhor the presenter. You play different roles with each other...and these roles may or may not have anything to do with who you are in the spiritual world. Know that. Believe that. Accept that. Life will be much easier for you if you do.

To reiterate: people play roles. No matter what role, how "positive" or "negative" the role, before incarnation you constructed the experience. What people do and say to you is not personal. It is simply a script *you* created to experience what you wanted in this lifetime. Don't take it personally. After all, you are the one who created your entire life. You also created "forgetting" your power once you incarnated.

Have you thought about who "directs" or "supervises" the movie or blueprint (using both metaphors) once you incarnate? The "who" is the crux of the issue.

Dear Ones, the "real" you, your Soul Self, is the director, the supervisor of the actor, the persona, in the movie. When you incarnate, you take on a role different from your true essence. You put on a costume and play the part you wanted to play. You wrote the movie. You worked with others to cast the various parts, even the extras. You set the scenery. Then you played the role. You needed a director, someone who has the whole script, who knows the theme and how it is to unfold in every act, scene and line. That role, precious ones, is filled by your Soul Self.

What is difficult to understand in this world of duality is that you and your Soul Self are the same. Think of your favorite actor. Does s/he quit being who s/he is when a particular part is played in a movie? The actor "steps out" of being him or herself and "steps into" his or her role. S/he must "forget" who s/he truly is to play the role.

You are still who you were before you took on the part. You are infinite. You are divine. You are a tremendous creator. Simply look at your life. You created everything in it. You just forgot all this so you could play your role of limitation to perfection.

You may be saying, "This is not a good creation. This is a disaster!" That is your judgment as the persona on this planet...the judgment you created for your movie. The truth is that your persona's judgment is not correct. You, an infinite being, created something in such detail that you believe you created a disaster. You did such a wonderful job of creating that you convinced this aspect of yourself, the persona you believe is truly you, that you and all that surrounds you is real. I have said, and you have heard many times, this life is not real. It is illusion. You created such a wonderful illusion that you convinced yourself there is no illusion, that you are limited and powerless. What power you have demonstrated by this amazing creation you call your life! How powerful you are!

Your Soul Self knows exactly what *you* (that's the "you" you think you are plus your Soul Self) wanted to create. Your Soul Self is managing everything from the fullness of itself. Your Soul Self has complete knowledge of what is happening "down here." (Now you understand there really is no "down here.") Your Soul Self watches you and manages all the little details of your life.

Let me explain how this might work. Let's say you, in your incarnated form, have had such painful knees that you choose to have a double knee replacement before you were 45 Earth years of age. You, in your incarnated form, may rage at this. You may throw yourself a pity party and expect everyone to join you. Your Soul Self is only assisting you in what you decided you wanted to do, remember, experience, and even play. *You*, the fullness of who you truly are, decided that your incarnated self wanted to play with the energies of having knee trouble. You experience having surgery accompanied by all the emotions, reactions and activities that result. *You*, the fullness of yourself, gathered the supporting cast to assist you: surgeons, nurses, therapists, even the experiences that set off the need for the surgery.

Your Soul Self is making sure that all you wanted to experience in this lifetime will occur. Those who might be considered "higher level spiritual beings" (which is a judgment, of course), may decide to play with the energies and experiences of being trapped in a life of drugs and alcohol. The incarnated experience, the role you take, never negates who you truly are.

Those reading this message wanted to experience what it was like to have access to different spiritual experiences. These experiences have been labeled New Age by some, the occult by others and, by yet another group, the devil's handiwork. Whatever you hear from others is your creation. The purpose is to cause you to respond in some manner. Whatever happens can precipitate a chain of events you planned.

Have you ever wondered why some people have powerful experiences with certain modalities, be they encodements, Reiki, affirmations, goal-setting, meditation, traditional Christianity, and so on, and you haven't? The "why" is a decision you made in the fullness of yourself before incarnation. Your job, as it were, is simply to experience life as it is. The "job" of your Soul Self is to implement the plan, direct the movie. Some will experience "results" using one modality, others another modality. Some will not be attracted to what is called New Age and others will be.

The concept of acceptance has been taught in many traditions by many teachers and masters. Does acceptance mean that you must simply do nothing? No. Although acceptance could be interpreted in that manner, it is more complex.

Acceptance requires discernment. Each of you will have strong desires to do something. This doing may be entering a relationship, beginning a business, taking a class, etc. Many of you can share experiences of taking a new direction in your life simply by following the deep inner urge to enroll in a workshop, attend a lecture or read a book. These deep urges are messages from your Soul Self. You could also say that the flier or book you saw activated encodements that propelled you in a new direction of your life.

Many of you are familiar with what is known as the Serenity Prayer: "God, grant me the serenity to accept the things I cannot change, the courage to change the things I can, and the wisdom to know the difference." "Wisdom," as used here, is about discernment. Wisdom is the discernment of when you act and when you accept things as they are, send love to others, or bask in the love that you are.

In this illusion of what you call your life you gain wisdom. You experience the illusion of learning from your experiences. (Remember, in Truth, you are an infinite being with infinite knowledge.) Learning in this manner is a developmental process just as learning to walk is a developmental process. The difference is that development in this area has extreme variations. Some people do not appear to learn from their experiences. Others learn very quickly. Realize you are experiencing exactly what you planned to experience, no matter the pace. This is where acceptance is key.

Your life is a balance of being proactive and of waiting for what comes to you. There are times when you will feel the urge to be proactive. Follow the urge. If following the urge results in what you would call disaster, it was all in the plan you made. You provided an experience for yourself. Listen. Feel. Experience. Make decisions based upon that which motivates you from deep within.

What about those who never learn this? Dear Ones, you are in the illusion of learning and experiencing. There is no "wrong" way to live this life. There are ways to live and experience that are judged to be healthier and happier. The truth is that there is no wrong way to live.

Does this mean you have a license to do whatever you wish? Yes, of course. Do whatever you wish and accept responsibility for the consequences you created. If you wish to steal then accept the responsibility of the consequences whether that is riches, fear or jail. You can choose what to experience in this lifetime. Your experiences will be in alignment with what you planned on experiencing. No experience changes the Love that you are.

Some will read these words and ask, "Why bother trying? Why bother growing?"

Developmentally, "Why bother?" is a question of adolescence. Think back to your own adolescence or to an adolescent you currently know. How can you convince him/her to stay in high school when s/he sees no value in high school? How can you explain that the process of high school, whether traditional or alternative education is more than "book learning"? Think of experiences you had or chose not to have and now regret. Your regret comes from what you learned by doing or not doing, from the wisdom you developed as you matured…again, all in the illusion.

Why bother living life? Generally, the answer is for the excitement, the wonder, the desire to see, feel, hear, and experience what will happen. What will be the ending of your movie? What will be the climax? Will things change if you do encodement work, holographic repatterning, Reiki, begin a new career when you are 50 or…. The only way you can find the answer is to live the question and watch expectantly. Those who have discovered the joy and excitement of learning for the pure joy of learning will understand this concept.

Those of you raised in the Christian tradition are familiar with the phrase, "Thy will be done." Within that phrase is the concept of trust and acceptance. Inherent in acceptance is trust in the One, the Being allowing and shaping the experiences coming to you. Also present is the challenge of living life to the fullest as it presents itself to you. "Thy will be done" has little to do with the nebulous concept of what many call God. "Thy will be done" is all about you, your Soul Self.

Through your Soul Self, you are able to access that which you call God...the undifferentiated Oneness. If you cannot access your being one with your Soul Self, you will not be able to embrace the truth of Oneness, of the concept of God, the All, All That Is. In a manner of speaking, your Soul Self is your bridge to the overarching energy of what many call God. Your Soul Self is the bridge between you and the powerful creative force that is Love Itself.

My Dearest Ones, your inability to be in an attitude of acceptance is related to your inability to trust yourself, your Soul Self. If you cannot trust your Soul Self, yourself, then you cannot trust that which you call God, All That Is, Universal Love, Allah. The reluctance, the fear, of trusting is held fast by the inability to trust yourself, your Soul Self. When you allow yourself to trust your Soul Self, when you move into true acceptance to the truth of "Thy will be done," you will discover the depths of yourself. You will discover the powerful creator you are.

Life on this Earth is filled with paradox. You created paradox because it is much more interesting than all the rules being static. You grow to know yourself, to enter into your power, only to realize that you have no power, and then enter into even greater power. The paradox is that you cannot experience even a hint of your true power until you find what you think is power and then realize you never had power. You learn to love yourself and set boundaries only to discover that a true love relationship involves the merging of boundaries and the releasing of part of yourself. The paradox is that you cannot release a part of yourself to another before you love yourself and establish boundaries. You cannot truly merge with another unless you first learn to be independent. Life is a continual tension between being proactive and accepting, moving forward and deliberation.

You planned every experience you have had, are having and will have. You planned a series of choices. If you made choice "A" you went in one direction. If you took choice "B" then you went in another. Your very first choice was whether or not to accept fully this incarnation, to accept life on this planet. Those who fully accept life have experiences built upon the wonder of acceptance. Those who do not, have experiences built upon the wonder of creating hardship. Many made this choice for or against life before they had the maturity to know the consequences of their choice, similar to the teenager who chooses not to finish high school.

The myriad of healing modalities in this wonderful world you created can assist you in making new choices. Healing the illusion of the past can change your present and your future. You will keep the wisdom with you. If you choose acceptance, "Thy will be done," you choose healing. You move in the direction that healing leads you. If you choose resistance you will go in the direction resistance leads you. Every person will end his or her incarnation by going "Home." That will not change. Everyone will make it "Home." Your choices now determine your experiences in this incarnation. This is what you planned. What experiences do you want?

If you have read this far into this message, your Soul Self is speaking to you, giving you an opportunity to move more deeply into the depths of consciousness. Take time to rest with the words I have given you. Allow yourself to be held in the dynamic tension of paradox. I, on behalf of your Soul Self, challenge you.

One last comment regarding another question: "Can what I planned before incarnation be changed?" The answer is, "Yes." In fact, it has already occurred. Anyone born before 1985 and still on the Earth plane has already experienced changes in the original plan. This change occurred, and continues to occur, on the soul level, the level of your Soul Self. You, in your human incarnation, are not fully conscious of these changes and their meaning. Where would be the fun and surprise if you already knew what would happen?

You are certainly able to have discussions with your Soul Self (see below). Realize that your Soul Self is the director of your movie. You are the star. You, in your human experience, do not have the wealth of knowledge and wisdom that your Soul Self has in infinite abundance. You do have access to knowledge and wisdom but only on a finite level. You created this to play the role of an infinite being "forgetting" you were infinite. The amount of access, however, may appear infinite when you access it. You can access it if you choose. Know that any difficulties in accessing this wealth of information are simply part of your story, your play, your movie.

Remember, you, as your persona, and your Soul Self are *you*. You and your Soul Self are the components of the infinite god-self that you are. The paradox is that you are an infinite being playing at a game in which you "forgot" you were infinite. As the vibrations of the planet have risen, the vague memory of who you truly are pokes through with the thought, "There must be something more!" You would not have this thought; you would not be reading this book, if you were not to know this information.

Remember the myths of drinking from the river of forgetfulness? You have forgotten from whence you came and who you truly are. You are, my Precious Ones, infinite. You are, as many of you have heard repeatedly, an infinite being having a finite human experience. The difficulty comes when you do not realize to the depths of yourself what this means. Relax, accept and trust. Then you can truly enjoy the play. You, also, will be able to hear the gentle whisperings of your Soul Self.

Now, for a few exercises to assist you in connecting with your Soul Self. Begin with whichever exercise you feel drawn.

1. Ask for the release of artificial encodements interfering with or inhibiting your communication with your Soul Self. If you are familiar with encodement work you may skip to #2.

As a reminder, enter into your Heart Source if you are not already there. Now go into the back of your heart center. Move deeply into this space until you come to your altar, your sacred space. Breathe in and out of your heart center. When you are ready, ask for the encodement technicians to come. They are there for the asking whether you feel them or not.

Ask if there are any artificial encodements interfering with or inhibiting your communication with your Soul Self. If the answer is "Yes" (a few of you will hear "No"), ask what would be the consequences of removing the artificial encodements. If those consequences are acceptable to you, then ask that they be removed.

2. Ask if there are damaged or altered natural encodements interfering with your relationship with your Soul Self. If so, ask that they be repaired.

3. Ask if there are natural encodements preventing your communication with your Soul Self. If the answer is "Yes," ask if their purpose has been fulfilled. If the purpose is complete, if you have experienced all you wanted, ask that they be removed.

4. Now rest in the energy of your Heart Source. Feel love surround you.

5. When you are ready, set your intention to form a clear connection with your Soul Self. Allow whatever happens to happen. Know that even if you do not feel, see, hear or sense anything, something is happening. Trust. Rest in the energy of this connection.

6. Ask for the healing of your relationship with yourself. Once you ask, be alert for healing opportunities. These could come through a book, an individual, an advertisement, a dream or an inspiration. Trust.

Cathy Chapman

7. Ask for the healing of your relationship with your Soul Self.

Again, be alert for opportunities of healing. Trust. As you do so, your power increases.

Revel in your increasing power as you activate and trust these simple exercises.

My blessings to you on this exciting journey of re-discovery.

———·—·———

Powerful Energy Centers

The Heart Source

You form the Heart Source through the following steps:

1. Enter into the back of your heart center.
2. Enter into the front of your heart center.
3. Enter into the front of your brow center.
4. Enter into the back of your brow center.
5. Connect your heart center with your brow center with a beam of light moving through your pranic tube from the heart center to the brow.
6. Move that beam of light up to the Center of the Universe (don't worry where that is).
7. Move the light to the center of the earth.

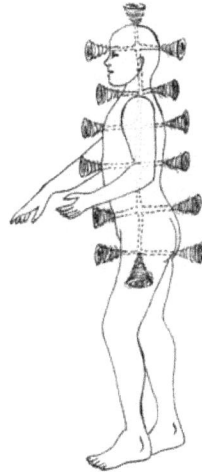

Remember, Dear Ones, you are infinite beings with tremendous power. You exercised that power when you made the decision to incarnate on this planet. Taking advantage of all your wisdom and knowledge, you decided what you wanted to experience in this lifetime. As you made your decisions, taking into account your past experiences (lifetimes) as well as your future experiences (future lifetimes), you put together a "team" of beings who wanted to share their experiences with you.

Remember this is all illusion even when I speak of it as truth.

From where you are right now, you have little idea of the complexity of this task. Imagine, you have thousands of actors who are planning their own play. They also agree to play various parts in the plays of others. Sometimes the parts are major and other times minor. At times, the part is simply background, extras. Can you even begin to manage the complexity of all these plays at the same time?

In addition, you have the being, Gaia, embodying this planet. There are the various living creatures that walk, slither, fly, swim, are rooted, or move upon the Earth in some manner. Each separate being has a consciousness with a purpose. All these innumerable consciousnesses and purposes are coordinated. Before reading on, attempt, as much as you can, to comprehend the complexities. Brain freeze occurs, does it not?

Now you have incarnated—at least you think you have. The truth, as discussed earlier, is that you as your persona are *an aspect of yourself* who has taken on a role and has totally forgotten who you truly are. You have forgotten you are an infinite being! Your Soul Self has not forgotten. Your Soul Self is enjoying the play you have written and are now acting.

The set of your play consists of a number of elements. There is the general set that is the planet Earth and all upon and within her. This includes plants, minerals, water, soil, and so on. Remember, they each have their own story. You each play a role in each other's story, but your story is not theirs, and theirs are not yours...in the illusion. Outside of the illusion everything is your story.

Realize that your Soul Self, which is you, is only concerned about your play. The only concern your Soul Self has about another's play is when it intersects with yours. You may ask, "Does my Soul Self have sympathy or compassion for others here on Earth?"

Dear Ones, does the director of a play have sympathy or compassion for the characters in the play? Sympathy and compassion are emotions that serve you on this planet, in this incarnation. They are needed by the director of your play only as necessary to keep the storyline progressing.

Your Soul Self is aware of all the various plays occurring on or in every planet. Your Soul Self can "watch" those plays at anytime. There is no sympathy because your Soul Self knows what is happening. Your Soul Self does not feel bad about your situation. Even in what you would judge the worst of situations and events, your Soul Self knows the reason and takes delight in how well you are playing the human game. Your Soul Self knows why things are occurring as they are.

Your incarnated self, your persona, whom you mistakenly believe is who you are, often experiences sympathy, even compassion, because you don't know the bigger picture. You don't know the whys and wherefores. You experience pain, as well as the pain of others. You're glad when that pain isn't yours. You experience sympathy, not wanting to share in the pain, because that is how life on this planet is created. That is how you created your play. Your Soul Self knows there is no pain; therefore there is no sympathy, or even compassion. In a way, your Soul Self does experience empathy because your Soul Self knows what is happening in your human experience.

Let's look at the other actors in your play. Some of them are aware of what many of you call the New Age. Some of your supporting actors play the roles of teachers and leaders in what you are studying and learning. Others give you support by challenging your beliefs and having you look closely at those beliefs. These people support you by giving you something to push against. In other words, those who appear to work against you are assisting the movement of your play. They are providing "strength training" by providing something to resist.

What I have been giving you in these teachings are various techniques to use in accordance with how your body is constructed. Your very body is a crucial part of your play. Your body is your costume for this incarnation. You have worn many costumes. You have played many parts. As you have played more parts in multitudes of lifetimes, your plays have become more complex in their interactions. The play you are in now, the set you have chosen for this play, is very complex.

How powerful you feel in this lifetime is determined by the information you have and how you use that information. Much of this information is in the form of belief systems. Know that you chose the belief systems you have just as much as you chose the parents, body, events and more that you have in your life.

Those who work in the counseling field in this wonderful illusion of yours are aware of the developmental statement that most belief systems are acquired before age five. That is true from the perspective of this incarnation. The truth is that you chose parents, situations, and supporting players who establish certain belief systems within you. This is how you created it all.

There are many healing modalities now available that will assist you in changing the energy of belief systems. You now know of encodements. We have touched on the energy field consisting of the aura, chakras and meridians. Many resources will assist you in gaining more information on these structures.

> *Your power manifests in direct proportion to how you use the information you acquire.*

As an example, the importance of diet has been proclaimed for decades. Many of you are unaware that when it was first proposed that diet could prevent heart disease, cancer, arthritis and many other dis-eases, the medical establishment laughed derisively at the concept. Notice how that is not true now! You may know about diet, but do you use the information? Your power lies in how you use the information.

I want to give you some additional information about the energy center that is in the physical heart. Yes, what you read is correct. There is a very important energy center that is a crucial part of the physical heart.

Picture your heart. Imagine dividing your heart into three equal parts—top, middle and bottom. Divide your top part into two equal horizontal parts. There is an energy structure that begins at the top one-sixth of the heart and extends an equal distance above the heart. This energy system is one-third the size of the healthy physical heart. (This heart energy center does not increase if the physical heart becomes enlarged.)

Although the physical heart energy system is connected energetically to the heart center or chakra, it has a different purpose. (Note: Since all is one, everything interacts with everything else. I have to use dualistic language here when there is no duality.)

The heart center (chakra) does have an effect upon the physical body. It needs to be open and clear for the physical body to "work" efficiently. The primary role of the heart center is with the energy body. The heart center is connected to the fourth auric level in the body. Even when I say fourth auric level, know that all levels intertwine or blend. They are not separate from each other.

The heart chakra will assist you in gathering inter-dimensional information and information in energetic form relating to the concerns of the fourth chakra. While in your fourth (heart) chakra, ask a question. Do that now. Go into your heart center and, when fully there, ask a question, any question, relating to your personal life. Jot down the answer. Now, go into your third (solar plexus) chakra and ask the same question. Jot down the answer. You can ask the same question from the place of each chakra. Gather all the answers and you will discover how the question is answered with the energy or filter of each chakra.

You will access different areas depending upon which aspect of the heart chakra you enter. You can travel through many dimensions, to various planets, and to many lifetimes through the back of your heart chakra. Entering through the front of your heart center will take you to adventures in this lifetime and to other people. If you wish to have a question answered that affects you in this incarnation, access the front. If you wish to have the question answered from an inter-dimensional perspective, enter the back. This applies to chakras two through six, which are the ones with a "front" and "back."

Now, let us return to the energy center in the physical heart.

Every organ and system in your physical body has an energy center where its consciousness resides. Every cell has its own energy center. You will recall that you can communicate with your body down to the cellular level through the individual energy centers of the organ or system. By "system", I'm speaking of the immune system, digestive system, lymphatic system, and so on. The energy center for a particular organ is contained within the organ. The energy center for a particular cell is contained within the cell. Those of you familiar with cellular biology know that each cell has its own physiological structure. Each one of those structures has its own energy center.

In regards to the various systems, there is an overriding energy pertaining to that system which governs the system. Communication with the system can be done by calling upon the energy of the system (e.g., I'd like to speak to the lymphatic system) or by focusing on the energy system of one of the organs that is part of that system. For instance, you can focus on the energy center of the spleen to communicate with the lymphatic system or you can focus on a particular lymph node or collection of cells with the intent of speaking with the lymphatic system.

The energy center of the heart is the governing energy center of the physical body. By this, I mean that focusing on the energy center of the physical heart has a direct and instant effect upon the energy centers of each part of the body. If you continually focused upon the energy center of the heart, you could bring the entire body into balance.

The heart chakra and the energy center of the heart have a direct connection with each other. If you focus on one, the other is equally activated. Yes, that means that focusing on the energy center of your physical heart will bring your entire energy system into balance as well as your physical body. Focusing on your heart center also brings both the physical and energy bodies into balance. Know, however, that this must be a continual focusing. This does not happen with a simple two-minute focusing. When you learn to live in your Heart Source, your body is able to remain in balance much easier and, thus, be healthier.

Some of you are asking, "Does focusing only for a few minutes help at all?" The simple answer is "Yes." As you begin to focus on either the heart chakra or the physical heart energy center, the physical and energy bodies begin to come into balance. The longer you focus, the more they will come into balance. Consider meditation. Meditating for two minutes does have an effect, but not the effect of meditating for thirty minutes.

Some of you are asking, "Does it matter which energy center we focus upon?" Yes, it does. Each energy center has a particular vibration for a specific purpose. If you focus only on the sixth chakra, or brow center, you will be primarily in your mental body. When you focus on your second chakra or sacral center, you will experience relationship much differently than when in your heart center. Focusing on your heart center brings all centers into balance.

When you are in a place of love and appreciation, your energy is focused in your heart area. Perhaps you have seen studies demonstrating that those connected to others and who have a spiritual connection appear to be, overall, healthier and live longer. This is because their energy focus is primarily in their heart. When focusing on this area, the physical and energy bodies stay in balance.

You have also read or heard much about the importance of living in the "now." Some call it mindfulness. When you are in the present, your energy is focused in your heart area. You cannot focus on the past or on the future for any length of time and stay in your heart area. Living in the now keeps you in your heart area which keeps your physical and energy bodies in balance.

Are you ready for some exercises on how to increase your power by using the energy center in your heart? To enhance the experience, move into your Heart Source.

Bring your attention to your physical heart. Set your intention to focus on the energy center that is at the top sixth of your heart and just above your physical heart. Notice what you feel and experience. Keep your focus there for a minute or more so that you can note changes. We will now work with certain organs and systems so you can understand how simple this is.

Keeping your focus on your heart, also focus on your liver. State your intention to connect with the energy center of the liver. You do not need to know where the energy center is. Setting your intention to focus on it is sufficient. Feel the connection between the energy centers of your heart and your liver. Hold that connection for a minute or more. Set your intention specifically (e.g., what you would like to occur with your liver) or generally (cleanse and balance).

The more you know of anatomy and physiology, the more specific you can be with your intention. For example, if you are aware of the Kupffer cells in the liver, you can set an intention regarding their relationship and their working together. To do this, focus on the energy center of the heart, then focus on the energy center of the liver. When that connection is strong (about a minute when you are first beginning), then ask for the energy center of the Kupffer cells of the liver. This energy center may appear to be more of an awareness or consciousness. Hold this three-way connection for about a minute to establish it firmly. State your intention. In this case, you could say, "Harmonize and balance."

If you know physiology, you can state the physiological reaction you wish, keeping in mind that what you think you know, even if you are an expert in the area, may not be correct. More is being discovered on a daily basis that is either refining or changing entirely what was first held to be true. Holding in mind the connections (heart, liver, cells) and making a general statement (harmonize and balance, cleanse and balance) would be sufficient. (You can also work with your encodement technicians while holding the energy connection.)

Let's say you are having digestion difficulties. Do you know the cause of the difficulties? Most people do not. It could be within your diet due to allergies or intolerances to certain foods. Surgery or another injury could have damaged the flow of the meridians affecting digestion. The difficulty could be in acid production, insulin production, antagonism between the stomach and pancreas, or any number of reasons.

For this example, we will use acid reflux as the difficulty. Although your pharmaceutical industry wants you to believe acid reflux is caused by too much acid, this is rarely the case. You might have too little acid for digestion. There may be a problem in the sphincter muscle between the stomach and the esophagus. You might have an overgrowth of Candida.

Focus on the energy center of your heart. Ask to connect to the energy center of digestion. You may feel your attention going to a certain location in your body or you may feel a connection with a consciousness. Hold within your consciousness your symptoms, something coming up from your stomach that burns, belching, bloating, etc. Feel the connection that you have established. Set your intention that all be balanced.

The above gives you a format for how to connect with various parts and systems of your body. You would do the same process for your glands and other body parts.

In addition to requesting balance, you can also request information. When connected to your digestive system, ask what it needs. Is there a particular food or supplement you need to add or eliminate? Do you need to change certain habits such as eating, drinking or sleeping? Get the information you need for yourself. One reason there is a proliferation of theories and philosophies is that no one answer fits everyone. Find out what works for you. The information in a particular book may fit you ninty percent, but the ten percent that doesn't fit may throw your system out of balance. Get the information you need from your body.

If you would like to gather complete information about your body, ask for information from each primary organ, each endocrine gland, each system, each body part, the cells, etc. Work with the areas in which you have pain or discomfort first. You can discuss the dis-ease with your body. Ask what brought you to the place of dis-ease and what can relieve the dis-ease. This will give you information you use for your own self-healing.

Information is power. Use the information and you can attain greater health. That which you know but do not use for your benefit, is a signpost of mental, emotional or spiritual issues that move your life in a direction that saps your personal power.

For those of you who facilitate healing in others, be it hands-on or distance, you can gain great insight into your client and gather information from your client's body, through a very simple exercise. Most of you know about connecting heart-to-heart with your client. Experiment with this process.

First, be sure you are in your Heart Source. Focus on your heart chakra and the energy center of your heart. Experience the connection. For some, this may take a minute until you feel, sense or see the connection. With practice, you will be able to do this simply with your intention. Now connect with your client's heart chakra and then the energy of your client's heart. From here you may connect with any part of the body, be it an organ, endocrine system or body part to the most minute cellular structure or process. Ask what you can do to bring balance to your client.

Using these techniques will increase your knowledge and your power.

Power Within the Illusion

I wish to emphasize that what I have been sharing, and what I will continue to share, is how you use power within the illusion. The fact that you are reading these words through your body is illusion, yet you experience it as being very real. What I share with you is how you can access your power within this illusion. Let us continue.

If you decide to kayak on a river, you would most likely choose to move down the river with the current. If you were hang gliding, you would go where you could catch the most favorable air currents. Whenever you are looking for the most efficient or easiest way to do an activity, find a way to move into the flow of the energy and allow the energy to carry you. If you go against the energy, you might still get somewhere. Your progress, however, will be much slower and more difficult.

Keep this in mind as I discuss astrological and numerological vibrations.

Let us talk about your astrology. First, remember that astrology is illusion. There are no planets or stars. There are no moons. There are no births or deaths. In the illusion which you have chosen to live, and I do mean the persona reading these words, you have created the planets, the stars, births and deaths to follow certain laws or structures. Since they were created by you, they can be manipulated by you.

It is no different from what you have seen in your government or how business or corporations run. The lawmakers make the rules and then spend time in seeing how they can manipulate them for those they wish. Your astrology here on this planet is based upon what you know as planets, stars and moons. As you have seen, your scientists have changed the rules and removed one of the planets. I say that with laughter as it is a perfect example of how you can change the illusion. As you have created it, there are forces within stars and planets and moons that play with each other. You may call them gravity or other names such as magnetic forces.

There are forces within your own body. All of those forces, within your body and outside of your body, play with each other. What most people forget in working with astrology or numerology is that this is all "consciousness." Consciousness is the one power or one force that is playing with all that you know. When astrology was first developed eons ago, observations and suppositions were made. It was the beginning of a new science.

These observations and suppositions began to form what is called a morphogenic field. The more people believed in them, the more they organized consciousness within this morphogenic field. Therefore, the organization of that consciousness became stronger and more structured. Belief systems began to be set, as you humans are wont to do.

All of this, Dear Ones, is due to the human need to believe there is a force outside the self. That belief is illusion. There is no force outside of yourself because there is no "self." If you believe in a self, then you believe in duality. Which, of course, you do, because that is the game you are playing.

My comments are based upon knowing that, in the illusion, you believe in duality and wish to understand this amazing force outside of yourself called astrology... which you created to play with. There are many books on astrology. I refer you to those yet I wish to make some general comments. By now, you are familiar with encodements. There are encodements for astrology.

When you planned your life before you incarnated, you also planned approximately when you would be born. Encodements were set for that time of birth. Most encodements for astrology were set in a range. For instance, a range could be that you would be born between September 1 and 15. The narrower the range, e.g., September 1 and 2, the fewer astrological encodements you had but they were more definite. For most people there is an activation of astrological encodements at the time of birth. This is true for any developmental encodements such as walking and talking.

In what I will call your modern age, just as you manipulate law, you manipulate birth. That is what happens when you induce labor and force a birth. When the birth has been forced outside of the range of encodements, you create astrological difficulties. (Remember, you created these events and these astrological complications.) Those of you who study astrology know that a small error or change at birth in plotting one's chart leads to great discrepancies over the years. Being born outside of the time for which your encodements were set is minimal at birth. However, as you grow and develop through the years, there begins to be a tension within you. For some, this tension prevents the ease and flow of life. For others, it is negligible.

Just as you can manipulate any law because it is in the illusion, you can manipulate encodements, which are also in the illusion. Let me give you a very simple exercise. While in your Heart Source, enter the back of your heart center and move deep within to your sacred space. Call upon the encodement technicians. Ask if the encodements you have for astrology need to be adjusted to the actual time of your birth. I am talking about when you were actually born, not the time on your birth certificate. (Clocks may differ, as well as when someone looks at the clock.) If you receive a "Yes," simply ask them to make the adjustments. The few who have known about this very simple request have experienced a greater ease in their lives.

Now, if you are a mother and your child was induced, you may do the same process for your infant. While in your Heart Source, go into the back of your heart chakra, standing in your sacred space, and feel yourself holding your child. Call upon your child's encodement technicians and ask if any encodements need to be adjusted and aligned to the astrological forces under which they were actually born. If the answer is "Yes," ask them to do so.

A very simple process, is it not?

I wish to make some general comments about astrology. Astrological influences are just that—influences. They are not determinative. There are better times to do certain actions according to the flow of astrology. However, if your boss tells you to begin a project when your astrological influences say that it is best for you to not begin a project, there are strategies you can use to please your boss. Simply call upon your encodement technicians to adjust your encodements to the astrological energies needed for you to fulfill the request of your boss.

Those of you who are very sensitive to the energies may feel a tension within you while this alignment is occurring. Within the illusion you are "forcing" the energies. Be sure to ask for a time limit in which this adjustment occurs so you are not constantly under this tension. This strategy pertains to anything you must do that is outside of what an astrologer may say is the best time.

There are those who blame the stars for what is happening in their lives, just as there are those who blame childhood wounds for what happens. I want you to know there is no difference between the two "blame-ings". They are both of victim consciousness. Anything within you is of the illusion, including childhood wounds and astrology, and can be changed.

Power is knowing it can be changed. The exercise of power is when you do what is needed to manifest that change. For example, if you know through your astrological charts that you have a tendency to sting people with your words or actions, be aware you have that tendency. Do not blame your doing so upon your astrology. Use the information as a signpost that here is something you need to transform. Become aware of what it is you do. Change your words and actions before they are manifested. Another example would be if you are aware that through your astrology your focus is more materially-bound, simply be aware of this fact as you connect spiritually.

Each sign, as most of you know, has its strengths and weaknesses as well as modes of transformation. Using this information will assist you in growing in all aspects of your lives. Being aware of the challenges and strengths of a particular time period will assist you in accomplishing more in your life.

All of this, Dear Ones, has to do with acceptance of what is, as well as making choices about what you would like. That is where your power is. You have the power to choose what you would like. You have the knowledge, or you can gain the knowledge if you believe it is not within you (an illusion), to change your actions and thought patterns. When you have the information and do not use it, it is simply your choice. There is no judgment about that choice—at least on my part. You may choose to see how this play of your life progresses with such actions and thoughts. If you wish to change the direction of your play, as in changing the third act, you have to change actions and thoughts to accomplish this.

In your illusion as you have created it, there are numerous galaxies and numerous universes. Each one of these is a force similar to your known astrology. Even if you are a master in the astrology of this planet, you do not have complete information unless you take into account the forces produced by other galaxies and other universes. I want you to see how you do not know all there is to know about these things that you believe determine your life.

You may gather information on other astrological forces by contacting those beings who are masters in this area. One way to contact them is, while in your Heart Source, enter your sacred space through the back of your heart center. Further ground yourself into the energies of this planet. You may do this in a manner familiar to you or follow your own guidance. Another simple method is to feel, see, or image your pranic tube as it comes into your crown, goes down your spine, and into the Earth. Follow the energy into the center of the Earth. Being grounded thus into the Earth energies provides you with the stability to travel into the nether reaches of the universe.

Now that you are grounded, ask to speak to the beings who work with the forces of the universes. Tell them what you would like to learn. The more specific you are, the more information you will receive. For example, if you are one who is very sensitive to the effects of the planet Mercury, you might want to know if there are any other influences that would strengthen or lessen the effects of that planet. You might also ask if there is something you can do to intensify or lessen the effects upon your energy. You may be given a meditation, mantra, name of a crystal or something else to assist.

There is much wisdom and knowledge available to you through your heart center. If you have a question about any area of your life, there are beings—not just your own personal guides— who can assist you. If you are puzzled by any problem, you can ask for the ones who are best able to help. When you go through the back of your heart center, while in your Heart Source, you will not only be able to access the higher vibration beings, but you will also be able to have more of the knowledge flow through you.

When I speak of the greater ease of flowing with the energies of the universe, I am not telling you that you must know astrology or have your own private astrologer. You may if you wish. There are those whose lives work wonderfully well without any knowledge or belief in astrology. These are the people who work from their hearts. I, and many others, teach the importance of being in your heart...and now I teach the power of being in your Heart Source.

When you are in your Heart Source, you are guided by the Oneness of which you are a part. When you are in your Heart Source, your thoughts and words are automatically governed by love. When you are in your Heart Source, your actions are automatically governed in the direction of love. When you are in the energy of love, which is in infinite supply within your heart, then your thoughts, words and actions are governed by that love. When you are in the energy of hate, then your words and actions are governed by the energy of hate.

Your power comes from deciding which energy you wish to reside within and then doing so. A decision without action is nothing more than an illusion within the illusion. There is no power in that.

Numerology is also about vibration. The world was created with vibration—with the Om. In ancient traditions, people were very careful to whom they revealed their names. Their names contained the vibration of their energy. Once you were aware of an individual's name, it was believed you had power over them. The power in knowing an individual's name is the power of having an entryway into their energy.

Numerology is a way of discovering the vibration of a person's name. The name on your birth certificate and the name you are called by those closest to you, have an effect upon your energy system. This influence begins as soon as your birth mother notices you are present. That which you are called sends a vibration into your developing energy system. Combine the effects of the vibration of that name with the energy vibration of how your name is used, (in distress, excitement, love) and the energy of this developing body in the womb will begin to be affected. Artificial encodements can be formed at this time as well as the altering or damaging of natural encodements.

When you are named, the numerology (vibration) of your name begins to interact with your energy, thus influencing your energetic vibration. As you mature, the name vibration becomes set more than when you were a child. Again, you can read about numerology in resources already available to you. I refer you to any of those resources to gain a basic understanding of numerology.

I wish to share with you now the basics of name change. When you become an adult—in other words, when you have been with one name for a long period of time—and you decide to change your name, perhaps through marriage, there will be a change in your vibration. If you choose to change your name for spiritual reasons, there will also be a change in your vibration. If you change by adding a title, such as Reverend, Doctor, Sister, etc., there is also a change in vibration.

The vibratory changes are increased when the name change is accompanied by a ritual, as in marriage, graduation or ordination. Many people, when they take a spiritual name, do so without the benefit of a ritual. Most people choose a spiritual name because they know on a deep level that their vibration has been changing as their spiritual energies have changed. They are drawn to a spiritual name that is more in keeping with their current vibration. If you wish to speed along this vibratory change, gather with some others of like mind for a ritual of your own developing.

Know, however, that the spiritual name you take is a spiritual name for this incarnation on this planet. It is not your "true" etheric name. On the other side, your name is a combination of light, sound and color, which you are not able to see or hear in this incarnational stage of development.

There are those who choose a different name because they have decided to choose a different life. To use a theme from movies, a gangster decides to stop being a gangster and changes his name immediately and drastically. The vibratory change will be a slow process and can be enhanced by a ritual.

Again, numerology is influencing. Vibrations do have an effect upon your energy body. They are not determinative. If you wish to change the way your life is going, work with the numerology of your current name. By current name, I mean that which you go by. Learn what is said about the numerology of your name. If it is not what you wish, and you have other names in mind, examine those numerologies. When you make the choice of a new name, even if you go from a diminutive such as Fran to Frances or Liz to Elizabeth, the vibrational change can be enhanced through a ritual.

You can also enhance the vibrational change by working with your encodement technicians and asking that your encodement system be aligned to the new vibration you have chosen. When you do this, ask if any artificial encodements from your previous name need to be de-activated. If so, have the encodement technicians do that. You will also want to be sure that there have been no damaged or altered natural encodements as a result of the vibration of your previous name. When I say this, I am not saying that the vibration of your name caused damage. I am saying that events, ways of behaving, thought processes in line with the vibration of your previous name, may have caused difficulties with the new vibration you wish to have.

Those who are going into business may wish to choose a business name in accordance with the numerology of the vibration that you desire for your business. For example, an accounting firm does not need the same vibration regarding change as a firm that works with the development of new products. There can be problems with creative accounting.

Again, numerology is not determinative. It is influencing. Choice is within your power. It is crucial that you recognize that power is within you. It is not outside of you. It is not in a god outside of yourself. It is not in the stars outside of yourself. It is not in the numbers outside of yourself. Your power is within you. When you place power in outside sources, you are abdicating your personal power. Those who abdicate their power have accepted the role of victim. You are not and never have been a victim. You may choose that role in this incarnation; however, that is not who you are. And not who you will be. You have within you the power of God in whatever highest way you define that God. You are Love Incarnate. You are nothing less than Love Incarnate. And there is nothing more than Love Incarnate on this planet.

Your journey in this incarnation is simply to experience being Love Incarnate. You play with the energies. You play with your choices. You play with your judgments. You have chosen to experience separateness in this incarnation. The truth is that you are not separate. The truth is you and I are the One, and I and you are the One. Any judgment you make about yourself or about others simply reinforces your belief that you are separate. The essence of detachment is to be without judgment. Without judgment, you are in the flow of Oneness. Know again, Dear Ones, and say this aloud now: "I (meaning you) am Love Incarnate". And therein is your power.

You Are the Power

My purpose in giving this information is so you will realize you are the power and presence of God. You are Love Incarnate. You are the power and presence of that love. You will discover this truth as you begin to accept who you are and as you fully begin to use the wonderful tools available to you. In your current incarnations on this planet, you convinced yourself you were not the power and presence of God, that you were not Love Incarnate. You convinced yourself that you are a limited being easily buffeted about by the chaos in the world.

Now you are discovering the amazing creation you are and how perfectly you created yourself to forget the truth of who you are.

I want to take a brief detour and show you how to work with encodements and your energy field.

Your physical body is structured from your energy field. When you have discordance in your energy field, eventually there will be discordance in your physical body. If your heart chakra or emotional center is closed, then you will eventually have problems with your physical heart, your cardiovascular system and anything related to the heart. You will also have trouble with relationships— true love relationships. If your heart center is closed, you are not able to open yourself to the fullness of another individual.

We have had discussions about encodements. As you know, encodements are energy structures. They affect other energy structures known as chakras, meridians, aura, central canal (also known as the pranic tube), and more. I want to remind you that when you have problems in a particular chakra you can ask if any artificial encodements are interfering with that chakra. (Those of you who work with energy healing can do this for your clients.) If artificial encodements are present, you can ask that they be removed. Do the same for damaged and altered natural encodements. If you are a healing facilitator, you will find it beneficial to do encodement work with any energy structure within you or a client.

You are an infinite being who has come here for a finite existence. In your finite structure, you cannot do all the things of infinity. You have certain limitations. For instance, those of you born female will learn how to experience a female life within your culture in a feminine body. If you are a male, you experience what it is to be a male in that culture, in that society. The only way this changes is if science intervenes and you have what is called a sex-change operation. Even if you change the physical body through surgical manipulation, you still grew up experiencing the other gender.

You will experience in your own way a particular culture. If a person of black color is born in a country that is predominantly black—Nigeria, for instance, s/he would have a different experience of being black than a black person born in the United States. The cultures are different. You make these choices before birth. You have natural encodements to assist you, e.g., if you're going to be in the United States, you will have encodements for that culture.

As you planned your life, you decided roles you would take such as a therapist, teacher, technician or parent. You have natural encodements moving you in the direction you planned. Remember, natural encodements are those placed within you by the encodement technicians, most placed before your birth.

Recall that artificial encodements are energy structures that comprise what some call thought forms. This means emotions, decisions or belief systems you form can change your energy structure. An artificial encodement can be formed by the energy of a decision or action by you or for you. Artificial encodements interfere with natural encodements.

When you have a problem in your chakras, aura or in any energy structure, you can ask if there are any artificial encodements causing the problem. You do that by talking to your encodement technicians. How do you get in touch with your encodement technicians? You go into the back of your heart center; go deep within until you come to what is your sacred space. Your altar is there. Everybody's altar looks different. This one I speak through has waterfalls all around her sacred space. Then you just ask to speak to the encodement technicians.

Once you have worked with your encodement technicians several times, you will not need to enter into the space within your sacred space. This process is to assist you in putting aside your thoughts and beliefs. Once you are comfortable in communicating with your encodement technicians, you call upon them and they will be present.

People experience the encodement technicians in different ways. They are beings who have never incarnated. They are not angels but are often experienced as angels. Most people have three technicians who come when called. However, at times there are more than three. Often there are two others, a master and an apprentice. When there are new or complex requests, a master comes to help facilitate the process. Before this time, encodements were rarely changed by request. Now that encodements are being changed consciously, don't be surprised if you have master technicians as well as apprentice technicians observing while you work with your personal technicians.

There are consequences to removing or changing your encodement system. Remember that when you are new at learning how to do this work, you may want to ask what the consequences would be of any change you request. There is often an influx of energy. Sometimes a barrier is removed and if someone is in a place of fear, s/he may fear the information or the energy that will come pouring in. In cases such as this, the artificial encodements may be removed gradually.

You may have developed such a defense system that you may not want to dismantle the encodements all at once. For instance, you may have artificial encodements blocking your heart center. You formed this structure around your heart center to protect you from energy coming in from the outside. When you suddenly remove that structure of artificial encodements, there will be an influx of energy. Even if that energy is of love, that love may be so startling to you, so alien to where you are that it could overwhelm you. You could withdraw and reestablish the structures. In this case, the incoming energy is too intense for you at this time.

Most people build a structure to protect their heart centers when they are very young. They grow up in situations in which they have to protect themselves from people who do not know how to love. Children come into the world open and, if they are attacked by energy that is damaging or overwhelming, they close themselves off. Artificial encodements, in this case, can be protective. They can be a survival mechanism. However, even though they may have worked well when you were five, they may not be supportive when you are an adult.

When you leave the situation that was damaging to you, you no longer need the protection. When you keep that protection in place, you are defending yourself against something that is not current. These defenses can then interfere with your current relationships.

The same is true for your belief systems. As a three year old you may develop a belief system that it is unsafe to express your true feelings because someone will make fun of you, berate you or even punish you. You develop a system to protect yourself. Your belief system could be "If I share my feelings, I will be hurt." That belief doesn't work well in relationships, does it? It was a survival mechanism as a child but it does not work well in an adult relationship. That is, of course, unless you choose not to share feelings and you are in a relationship with someone who also chooses not to share feelings. The difficulty comes when you move toward growth and healing. You begin to remove those blocks to relationship. You are ready to relate on a deeper level, a more honest and feeling level, and the other person is not. Ah, the complexities of relationship.

You can ask for the removal of the artificial encodements which anchor blocks within your heart center or heart chakra. It would be helpful to ask what would happen if you removed all of these at once. There will be times when the encodement technicians will absolutely not remove all of them at once. They know it could decompensate your entire energy system and cause more trauma.

You can ask how many of the artificial encodements or what percentage can be safely removed. Using percentages, you could ask if it would be best to remove ten percent once a week, for example. They may respond that is a good number to remove. That will give you a week to acclimate to the new experience. There have been those who have removed artificial encodements as little as ten percent once a month because their fear has been so great they needed time to adjust to the new energy.

Ask if you need to request the next removal of artificial encodements or if the technicians will just automatically do so. It will depend upon the person but, most of the time, they will continue to remove ten percent once a week or once a month, or whatever you have decided. If you feel yourself getting stronger and becoming more comfortable with life, you may want to tell them to go faster. Just reconnect with your encodement technicians and ask if you would be able to handle removing the artificial encodements at a faster rate. In many cases, if not most, the answer is "yes". By the time thirty to fifty percent have been removed, the next step could be to remove all of them. Because you've already removed so many, you have become acclimated to the energy and are opening up to the higher vibrations of light energy.

When you first start working with encodements, you may notice you sleep more. This is due to the tremendous amounts of energy expended in this work. Your body is telling you it needs a chance to acclimate. In addition, you are being re-calibrated. Your body was put into a place of relaxation. When you have done tremendous physical exertion, does your body not wish to rest?

People do not realize that simply asking for a change in their energy system takes much energy. Your physical body will want to rest to replenish itself.

For some of you, to get your conscious mind out of the way, the spiritual beings who work with you put you in a state of sleep. You may think that doesn't work very well when you have work to do, jobs to go to. I must tell you, Dear Ones, that your work in the world isn't nearly as important as doing this spiritual work. I can already hear those who are saying they might be fired if they don't go to work. Well, maybe being fired is the best thing for you.

You may find a desire to eat different foods. You may find a desire to take different supplements. An off-hand remark by someone about a new supplement may be intended as a message for you. Someone else may see coconut oil in the store and have a deep desire to buy it. Listen to your inner knowing respond to these messages.

Listen when something new pops up and ask if this is a message for you. Listen—even if what somebody says is what you judge to be negative, or said with a negative voice. Ask, "Is that meant for me?" "Meant for me" would be on a spiritual level, taking you deeper within yourself.

Most of you know the concept of mirroring, where for example, somebody very angry may be mirroring anger within you. When you see that situation, go inside and ask your Soul Self if there is anger within you that you need to release.

You may feel emotions changing inside you. That can be stressful. Be sure to get the rest you need during this time as your energies are regrouping. As you work on changes and your energies shift, you will notice that you are becoming a new person. Those who know you will notice. You may also use this process with belief systems. There are many powerful techniques to change belief systems. When you come upon a belief such as "It is unsafe to share feelings," you may ask that the encodements holding that belief system be removed. This is where we have more complex encodement work.

Let's say you came into the world with the encodements that it is safe and good to reveal your feelings. That was your belief system.

Something happened in life and an artificial encodement developed which said that revealing feelings is unsafe. Just ask the simple question, "Are there any artificial encodements holding in the belief that it is dangerous to reveal feelings?" If you get a "Yes" answer, ask what the consequences would be if they are removed. You may want to ask what would happen if all of them were removed at once. If you get, "extreme fatigue" or something similar, you can ask what percentage can be removed in order for you to function at work and at home. Your encodement technicians may say, "You can function very well if you remove fifteen percent right now. Every Friday, you may want to remove another fifteen percent." You do not need to understand how the process works. In the same way, you do not need to know how a carburetor works to start your car. What I'm giving you are simple guidelines. You do not have to know the intricacies of encodements. If you were to become a healer who would work with them, it may behoove you to know a bit more. Even then, there is no need to complicate it by having to learn all the details.

If someone hands you this book and says, "This book contains the key to your health." You know that might be true because people who read this book and use the information in it often become healthier. The book serves you no purpose if it just sits on your desk. You have to pick it up and read it. Even then, it does you no good unless you do what it says.

The same is true in working with the encodement technicians. You simply need to ask. All you have to do is to ask the encodement technicians to help, and they will help you. Other healing techniques also change encodements. It does not happen directly so you are not as aware of what is happening. Another person helping you with your healing can also connect with your encodement technicians and ask that this work be done. You do not even need to know what they are doing. By going to a healing session, you have given the healing facilitator permission to work with you in ways that move you to growth.

If there is someone you have anger towards because you believe they've hurt you, you can do encodement work to remove artificial encodements holding that anger in place. When you see that person again, look into his or her eyes and see them as Love Incarnate. If you choose to see them as the one who hurt you, then you are the one wounding yourself again, and the artificial encodements return through the choice of your actions. You made a choice to stay in a place of anger and resentment.

You can prevent artificial encodements from returning by choosing to release low vibration energy and staying in a place of openness, love and acceptance. You can transform someone's behavior as you release more and more. It is amazing how that happens.

You may ask, "How do I do that?" if you have someone saying negative things to you. Instead of taking in the energy of that hurt, if you remain in your Heart Source, staying deeply within your heart, your energy will expand and the energy of their words will not come into you. At the same time they are saying those words to you, you can repeat a mantra or phrase of love. For example, you could be saying, "She is Love Incarnate. She is Love Incarnate. This person is Love Incarnate." The energy of these words keeps you in your heart and strengthens your energy field. You are better able to fend off the low vibration energy coming from others.

It is the energy you allow to enter you which causes the problem. If you encounter someone who sucks your energy in a negative way, there is no reason to be with them, even if they are family. There is no reason for you to be with anyone who depletes your energy field, unless you so choose.

What happens if you must be in an energy depleting situation…caring for a sick loved one, for example? Stay in your heart. Send love from your heart to the other. Repeat the words, "You are Love Incarnate. I am Love Incarnate." Ask for the removal of artificial encodements on a daily basis at minimum.

Another technique would be: Go deeply within your Heart Source, expand your energy around you, stay in your heart center, and ignore what someone is saying to you. Your heart center is the most powerful energy center you have. This is the center where transformation can occur. When you stay firmly within your heart center and you send the message to others that they are Love Incarnate, then your mind and heart are occupied with focusing on Love Incarnate. You are not occupied with fending off the energy they are sending you. This is a bit of a paradox. You are not occupied with fending off the energy; you are occupied with sending the energy. Their negativity will not affect you. It takes great strength and focus to do this. Everyone has the responsibility to protect him or herself. There is no responsibility to protect others unless you have the responsibility of children and the infirm. Even then, you are not responsible for protecting them from everything that could happen. That would be impossible. Your responsibility lies in giving the basic care and love they need.

Is there anything wrong with trying to protect others? You have flown in an airplane? Who gets the oxygen mask first? You cannot help another person, be it a child or panicky adult, if you do not put on your oxygen mask first. If you do not protect yourself first, you cannot help other people.

Remember that artificial encodements can originate from your own thoughts, your own feelings, from what you read and hear, even from what you eat. For instance, genetically modified food can cause artificial encodements. Traumatized animals and pesticides can cause artificial encodements. Anytime during the day, but especially at night, you can simply ask your encodement technicians to remove all artificial encodements you acquired that day. Think of them as dust you pick up during the day and release at night. You can do it while taking a shower or a bath. Make it a habit to ask for the removal of any and all artificial encodements you "collected" during the day.

To live your life to the fullest in any situation, learn to stay in your heart. Do not misunderstand what this means. Staying in your heart does not mean you are opening yourself to the energy of everyone around you.

Your Heart Source is your most powerful tool in protecting yourself. When in your Heart Source, you fill yourself with the high vibration love energy contained in the heart. The low vibration energy coming towards you either "bounces off" you or is neutralized. When in your heart you have a feeling of well-being and joy that not only attracts some people to you, but also forms a higher vibration shield around you, protecting you from the low vibration energies of others.

The energy of someone extremely negative may attempt to break through your shield. Your job is to stay in your Heart Source and make no judgments about others. A judgment can lower your vibration opening your energy to more negativity. Your power is in your decision to remain in your Heart Source no matter what the other person says or does. Stay in your heart when you know you are going to be with family members who are so wounded they automatically respond with negativity, who are so wounded that your presence threatens them in some way. People do not give out negativity unless they are threatened. Fear is the result of being threatened. Fear is not-love. Stay in your heart to prevent yourself from entering "not-love."

Access your power by using the tool of your Heart Source. From your Heart Source expand the energy around you. Another tool is speaking the truth about the individual. The truth is that he or she is Love Incarnate. Do not accept his or her own lie about the self. The illusion of non-love seen in the emotions of anger and fear is not their true nature any more than it is of you when you are in a negative phase with someone.

When you are depressed, that is not who you are. That is what you are experiencing at that time. It is total illusion, a creation on your part to play this human game. Who you are is Love Incarnate. Focus within your heart and stay within your Heart Source, no matter how difficult it may be—just as it is difficult to do weight training or to increase stamina by swimming laps in the pool. You must practice. Practice staying in your Heart Source. Do this until staying in your Heart Source becomes how you live. Continue to practice this fundamental state of being.

When staying in your Heart Source, you will find that you attract more happy people to you. You may also find, especially within family, there are some who are jealous of you. They may attempt to bring you down because they cannot tolerate your happiness.

When you are in your Heart Source and proclaiming in your mind the truth about that person, they are Love Incarnate, they cannot harm you energetically. This means your physical body is protected because your cells vibrate in unison with love. When your cells do not vibrate in unison with love, then biochemical reactions occur which weaken your body. The transport of different minerals across the cell wall becomes distorted, as well as the DNA/RNA. The protein sleeve around the DNA/RNA moves and changes. The vibration of the cells changes weakening the cell wall.

The key is to be in your Heart Source and stay within your Heart Source 24 hours a day. That is what your spiritual masters do. They live there 24 hours a day. You have these people who are able to relate, see and be with people for hours and seem to have no stress. It is because they are staying within their Heart Source. Your power lies within you.

If you were able to stay within your Heart Source, you would not need encodement technicians, you would not need supplements, you would not need nutrients, you would need nothing. By being in the deepness of your Heart Source, everything will begin to heal, including your emotions. The belief systems you may judge as negative will begin to fall away into the belief systems you wish to live within your life. When you are in your Heart Source and you are sending out the vibration of love energy, your whole body will respond because it was created in love.

Moving in your Heart Source is simple. Remaining there can be difficult. This is because your world is filled with low vibration energy bombarding you, weakening you and lowering your vibration.

How do people make the most money? Isn't it by using the emotion of fear? Be aware of this. Is most of the advertising based on joy? Or love? Much is based on sex, but without love. There is fear of aging, fear of illness, fear of somebody breaking in, fear of somebody blowing up your plane, fear of someone leaving you, and on and on. All of that fear assaults your energy which deteriorates your body. You counteract fear by staying in your heart.

Advertising is also based upon greed. Greed is a low vibration energy. You can desire to have something because it is fun and joyous to have. This is not greed. When you have to have something so you will feel better than another, or to prove to the outside world you are successful—that is low vibration energy.

I'll show you how to strengthen your protective energy even more.

If you are in your Heart Source, these steps will strengthen your connection…with a little addition.

Go into your heart center from the front and from the back. You can do this—just bi-locate your energy. Enter into the back of your heart center and move towards the center. Now enter the heart center from the front and move towards the center. You do not quite meet in the center because you are in two different dimensions.

Have the intention that the energy expand. Feel it expand. Feel it expand around you. While remaining in your heart, become aware of your solar plexus chakra. Go into this third chakra from the front and the back. Feel the connection between your solar plexus and your heart chakra. Just feel that connection moving upward. Feel what happens. Feel the strength that comes. Do you not feel even more solid?

Hold that energy and go into your second chakra, the sacral chakra, front and back. Feel the strength of that energy. Stay in the other chakras while you do this. Now, with intention, connect your second chakra with the others we've connected. Continue to expand your energy. Feel what happens to you.

Now connect all this energy to the first chakra at the base of your spine. Keep it all together. Feel that energy fill you.

Now, drop a line of energy from the first chakra at the base of your spine down into the center of the Earth. Request more energy from the Earth. Whatever amount you need will come. Feel it moving upwards. Feel it filling your first chakra…your second chakra…your third chakra…your fourth chakra.

Enter now into your throat chakra, front and back. Connect that chakra with the others. Let the throat chakra energy expand so that it is fully connected with the others. You might feel tingling in your body, in your hands or feet.

Now go into your sixth chakra, your brow chakra or third eye. Go into it front and back. Feel the expansion and connect with the other chakras. Feel how much stronger you are; how much more you are in your body. Your energy field is expanding and expanding. It is many feet beyond you.

Connect now to your crown chakra. Expand the crown. If you feel a little headache, it doesn't matter; it will go away. Notice there is a beam of energy coming from above, down into your crown chakra, going down your spine and all the way into the center of the Earth. Feel that energy.

Set your intention: Chakras spin. Include in your intention that they spin in the exact direction you need. Feel what happens. Can you imagine walking out into the world like this? Going to work like this? Meeting your family like this—especially those who cause problems within you?

I want you to imagine, right now, the individual you have the most difficulty with in your life; it could even be yourself. Imagine that person standing in front of you. Stay in the energy within your heart. Just stay in your heart. Be conscious of the energy around you—how expanded you are and how strong you are. And now, to the person you have placed in front of you, simply say in your mind, "You are Love Incarnate." Feel what happens to your energy. Now say, "I am Love Incarnate," speaking to yourself. "I am Love Incarnate. You are Love Incarnate." It does not matter what they are saying to you. That energy cannot penetrate you, unless it is the energy of love.

See how long you can stay in this space.

You could practice this every day, as many times a day as needed until you are able to realize when you are not in your Heart Source and return there, connect with every chakra, and expand yourself. With practice, you can connect your chakras and expand them in an instant. When you are in this state, do you know that if you accidentally hit a table, you won't even bruise? This is because your energy will protect you. Amazing, isn't it?

This is a very simple exercise. If you stayed in this space for 24 hours a day, your body would begin to heal. At first, you would be tired because, during the adjustments, your body would begin to release toxins. Being in your Heart Source, connected to all other chakras, activates your power.

The following are answers to some pertinent questions people have asked:

Q: *How much faster do we age because of the encodements we have?*

A: The artificial encodements? You age greatly because of them. Your belief systems age you tremendously. Some will say you could live 100, 150, 250 or even 500 years. Your body is self-replicating.

Q: *What about using youthful hormones?*

A: Youthful hormones are an illusion just as the body is an illusion. If you accept the belief these products will help, they will assist you somewhat. I can tell you that unless you learn to love yourself and others their effect is temporary. What I have just taught you is the best way to stay youthful and strong as long as you are playing in this illusion.

Q: *It lines up your energy, doesn't it?*

A: Yes, it does. When your chakras are all in balance, it will also expand into your meridians and your aura. Remember that we brought in the energy from above and from below. It connects with your central canal and other structures such as your hara line, which also comes from above and below. It contains your incarnation. It also connects with your core star, your soul seat and your personal individuation point. There are other little structures within the aura that very few people know about. You do not have to know the details or the intricacies of these things.

No matter what another may do to you, the energy of the words or actions cannot befoul your spiritual energy. Could someone kill your physical body? Of course, but you are not your physical body. You will be stepping out of these "clothes" at some point anyway.

Q: I believe that the body is always poised to heal at the minute we have the right focus and right attitude. That's how we acquire our remarkable recoveries, whatever the disease. Would you comment on that?

A: Your saying, it is "poised to heal" is exactly what I have been talking about when I say to stay within your heart. You cannot heal from your head. You have to connect your head to your heart. You can convince yourself of certain things and you could heal temporarily. But that healing may not continue if you stay out of the focus of your heart. Your body is made to respond to the vibration of love. Anything that is not of the vibration of love is a vibration that will counteract what the cells need.

Those who are able to subsist without food or water stay within the vibration of love. They also work with the energies from the sun. They learn how to incorporate those energies within them which sustains their bodies. It is a belief system that you need food and sustenance. Nothing you can put into your body can damage it *if* you believe your body can assimilate all it needs and discard the rest…and if you stay within your Heart Source.

Q: Are the people who do this for show able to get into that space and then, after that event is over, shift into their "normal" space?

A: Let's take the simple example of those who do fire-walking. When they are in that special space while walking on the coals, they are not burned. Yet, when they are out of that space, and they should accidentally step on a hot coal at the side, most of the time they are burned.

Let's go back now to the other energy structures. I'd like to talk more about them. You will recall I've told you that the hara line comes from above and goes down through you, and it contains your incarnation. It can be damaged in many different ways—falls, accidents, etc. This one has had that happen to her. She was in an automobile accident and had a very difficult time getting back into her body. A friend did some energy work with her and discovered that her hara line was broken. Here is a way to fix a damaged hara line.

Ask if there are artificial encodements preventing the hara line from coming together. Have those removed. You can also ask if any of the natural encodements were damaged or altered and are keeping the hara line from repairing. Ask that they be repaired.

Here is something new that I haven't shared before. You can ask that the encodements be matched up so that the hara line will be brought back into one straight line. Encodements can be in pairs or sets that are to align with each other.

You can do this with your soul seat and your personal individuation point. You can do this with parts of your aura. For instance, when someone's aura is bigger on one side than the other, you can ask if there are artificial encodements causing the distortion.

Hopefully, you are getting the message that you can use the encodement process with almost anyone and anything. If you have a pain somewhere, you can ask if there are artificial encodements contributing to that pain, and have them removed. Artificial encodements can be preventing healing in a particular area of the body. Belief systems can be involved. There can be layers upon layers upon layers of beliefs affecting you.

Power in Relationships

As I share with you this message, your encodement technicians will be working with you and on you as we talk about relationships.

As you read this information, remember you are an infinite being. You are Love Incarnate. You came to this earth to play the human game of limitation. Relationship is one of the primary games where you convince yourself you are finite and limited.

Know that the message I give you is about playing in the illusion. The words may sound as if I believe all you are experiencing is real. This world you experience is only illusion. It is only a set design or stage to play this human game. Everything I say, except when speaking the truth about Oneness, is illusion…even if it sounds as if I'm speaking of it as real.

Now, to the discussion on the relationship game …

Nobody reading this has ever had any problem with relationships, have you? (Chuckle)

What's amazing about difficulties with relationships is that, metaphorically, it is the same as your hand and your foot, or your heart and your liver, not getting along. Your body consists of many relationships within the Oneness itself.

When you have relationship problems, you are having difficulty with an aspect of yourself because all is Oneness. You may think, "How could this person be one with me when there has been violence, anger, complete misunderstanding, and pain?" You can recognize the Oneness when there is excitement and joy. You understand the Oneness when in that state, do you not? Yet there is Oneness in the pain, also.

I'd like to talk about power in relationships and how you can assist yourself in relationship. I'm sure you all have heard of the concept that you incarnated to learn certain things. You say that frequently. But the truth is there is nothing for you to learn. There are, however, infinite experiences to be had. You are an infinite being, are you not? You are Love Incarnate. What is it that you think you have to learn? What does an infinite being have to learn?

You came here to experience, to play with certain energies. You came, not because you had to, but because you wanted to. So, you are saying to yourself, "Well, I did not want to have this kind of difficulty in relationships." Few people on this planet have smooth relationships with others. No one has a smooth relationship all the time. Think of the ones you are closest to, your children, your spouse, good friend, think of the one who tried to run you off the road. All relationships are in the Oneness.

Remember the encodement technicians are working with you to process what I am saying on this three-dimensional level as well as on the deepest part of yourself, your soul level. They are assisting you.

The first thing to realize is there is no thing, nothing, outside of yourself that has power over you.

That's hard to imagine, isn't it? When someone goes through a red light and hits you, it's difficult to accept that you planned that. It is not that you asked for it in a pejorative way. It is what you decided to experience in this lifetime. You included it in your script! You wanted to experience how an infinite being could forget being infinite by becoming finite. You are finite now. You have set out to discover your way back to your infinity. An interesting process, is it not? You do not need to know anything else on your soul level. It is all about being here in this world, having experiences and seeing what you would do. That's all it is. Your life really isn't about lessons.

You may be playing a new game in this lifetime. You may be playing the game of Risk. Has anyone played that game? Or Monopoly? Or Chess? When you are learning those games, you learn the rules applicable to the particular game. The same is true of the human game. With each incarnation, you experience a different game.

Before coming to this planet, before incarnating, everyone you know came together for a planning session. You each chose the role you would be playing. All of you made an agreement to be here at this time, in this place. You chose to experience what it is like to find your way when the street is blocked, to experience what it is like to discover things as you are surfing the internet. You are playing the human game in the historical time period of the Twentieth and Twenty-First Centuries. It feels very serious, doesn't it, as you struggle with life and death issues as well as with the bodies (physical and energetic) you are wearing?

It is difficult to remove yourselves from the belief system that life as you know it ends when the relationship with your body ends. One of your first relationships is with your body. Think about that relationship. If I asked you to think about twenty things you do not like about what you've experienced in your body, how quickly could you make that list? Most people could do so very quickly. If I asked you to think of twenty things you thoroughly enjoyed in this body of yours, is that a more difficult list to develop?

For most people, it is. They often forget the feeling of being at the beach, for instance, with their toes in the sand and the breeze on their face. Or they forget about a time when a little two year old came up and grinned and said, "Hi." An experience like that warms the heart, does it not? How about your most memorable sexual experience?

There is nobody who likes his or her physical body completely. You may say, "But I do like it." Then I will ask you, "Are you on a special diet...or think you should be?" Most likely, your answer will be, "Yes." Well, then you either don't like your physical body one-hundred percent or are afraid of what could happen to your body. You may say that if you don't eat the correct foods your physical body will not work well. That can be true if that is how you are playing the human game with your body...and many people are doing so.

Are you exercising? Then you don't like your physical body as it is...or you are in fear of what could happen. I am not making a quality value judgment here. I'm trying to point out that whenever you attempt to change things, it is because you do not like them or are in fear of something else. And that includes your physical body.

What would happen if you said, "I love my physical body. Because I love it I'm exercising in the way it wants and eating what it wants." That is different than attempting to change your body.

It is important to realize that your liking things about your body—the food it enjoys, the way it looks, the shape of it, the strength it has, the color of its hair, having hair or not having hair, and any other issue—came from people around you. Without others' views about your body, you would not know there was anything to like or not to like about it. You know the remarks: "You're putting on weight." "You're so skinny." "I could really help your hair color." "Poor thing, you have your father's nose." People outside of yourself tell you about your physical body.

When you grow up, society begins to tell you how appropriate your physical body is or isn't. This often begins with your siblings. For instance, if your older sibling can climb up and get the cookies and you can't because you are only crawling, you begin to develop a relationship with your body that says, "I can't do that." Then you either strive to do the same or give up and become resigned that you can't.

Even at that very early stage, you begin to develop a belief about your physical body—your first relationship with yourself. You begin to learn and to know that your physical body is who you are. And that is not true. Your physical body is not who you are. But you begin to develop a like or dislike of yourself based upon what you and others think and feel about your physical body. How many people do you know who go into great angst because their physical body is not the way they think it should be?

When you were very little, you established a relationship with your caregivers, usually with a mom and a dad. If you're adopted, the relationships are more complex because you have biological, foster and adoptive parents. Let's speak of it in a simple context—the relationship with those who have raised you.

You begin to have a relationship with someone outside of yourself. At an early age, you begin to know there is another being who wants to have a relationship with you. Even in the womb, you can sense that it is important to the one carrying you that you live and be successful…or that they wish you weren't there. Sometimes women are not happy about being pregnant, especially during those first difficult months, and then they come into the joy of having a child. Those first thoughts about not being comfortable having a baby can have lasting effects. This depends upon the strength of the thoughts held within the cellular memory of the child.

The encodement technicians are working with you in this area right now to remove artificial encodements that have come from the birth mother being concerned about carrying the child (you) or the father not wanting you. Just know this is happening at this moment.

With those first relationships you learn what it means to please someone in power. Parents are your first power figures. They are your first god. You believe that a parent has total power over you. Since you were born you were unable to turn over, to feed yourself or clothe yourself. A parent appears to have that god-like quality of total power. You, who have forgotten you are an infinite being, begin to believe someone outside of yourself has power over you. As an infinite being, no one has power over you, but here you are convincing yourself that someone does.

As you grow, you discover other people have power over you—babysitters, doctors, teachers, and other authority figures. Your personality begins to develop. Some of you begin to believe you are powerless in every way. You become shy and fearful. Some of you become bullheaded and determined to let no one control you…not even to teach you good things. You become tenacious and stubborn, or even a bully, when exercising your power. These patterns begin very, very young.

You begin to have friends. Your first friends when you are two or three years old are very important to you. You will hear scientists say that little ones can't form friendships at that time. That is not true. Just as the scientists were wrong when they said as long as you were raised in a loving family, it didn't matter if you were adopted. What happens those first nine months is crucial. And your first friendship is crucial. Even as a toddler, you begin to learn whether it's safe or unsafe to have relationships.

You may feel something going on inside of you right now. That's because your encodement technicians are doing some work in this area for you.

Then you begin this thing called school, whether it is pre-school, kindergarten, or first grade. When you are four, there are things you don't want to do. Think about that. If you are in pre-school, there will be a time when you can play with your blocks and there will be a time when you can't play with your blocks. There will be a time when you want to draw—and they want you to play with your blocks. You begin to learn there are times you cannot do what you want. You learned that at home but now you are learning it more thoroughly in a group. You call it socialization.

Even though there is truly nothing outside of yourself because of the Oneness, in your finite-ness, you have learned there are others outside of yourself who relate to you. Some like you and some don't. Aren't there people whom you are immediately attracted? And those who immediately repel you? One of the most difficult events for someone is that first time they are deeply drawn to someone…and that person does not return the feeling; or the time someone is drawn to them…and they don't return the feeling. All of you have had similar experiences. It sets up within you a sense of powerlessness and a belief you cannot be in control.

What I wanted to show you is how, from the very beginning of life, you come to believe you have no power. This is not the truth, but it is how you are playing the human game in this particular incarnation. You set it up to adapt to what other people want.

Let's talk now about adult relationships. Those of you who have children know that when they are very young, you have control over them because you are god to them. Then they reach that age where they believe you are too old to know what life is really like. Think about that. Think about your own life back in that teenage world when you thought your parents didn't know anything. Then in your twenties, or maybe early thirties, you were amazed at how much wisdom they acquired.

There comes a time when you decide to declare your independence. This is one of the major battles in relationship. You decide what it is you want to do and what you don't want to do. The other person gets to decide if they are going to let you do what you want, or not. As a parent, you may want to mold your child to be happy and self-sufficient, to find someone to live with whom he or she loves, and to give you wonderful grandchildren. The difficulty comes when your parents' ideas of success and whom they wish you to live with are different from your own. This is made more difficult when the two parents disagree. Who are you going to please?

How can you manage such situations?

Think about a relationship you now have where you feel you're beating your head against a brick wall. Have somebody in mind? You might have great fear for them or you might have great fear of them. How do you handle that situation? Do you feel powerless to change what is happening? Relationships can keep you from feeling and experiencing your power because you have created having no power over others.

What I'm going to share with you are rather simple strategies. They are not easy.

First, realize that no one outside of yourself can have power over you—not a parent, not a spouse, not a partner, not a friend, not a child no matter how old s/he is. You can make decisions for your life in any way you wish to make them. You may devise many reasons or excuses of why you cannot do that…and that is a choice.

You may say that it is not right or it is wrong to do this...and that is your choice.

It may seem strange for many of you in the way you were raised, but there is *no right or wrong*. There is no infinite being for whom you have to do things in order to gain approval. You ARE that infinite being who came here to experience limitation.

There are things that usually make life easier in this incarnation because that is how you set it up. Let's say you are not happy in a particular job and would really like to be out of it. If I were to tell you to get out of that job, you might say that if you did, you wouldn't know where the money would come from or if you could find another job. You would be overcome with terror or fear because you don't know what is going to happen next.

You think that you are going to be powerless...the belief that you are a finite being. It does not really matter whether you have a job or not. You may think that what you would like to do in this lifetime is to eat, have clothes and a place to live other than beneath a bridge. That may be what you believe, but the truth is that it doesn't really matter. You create the things and events you desire to experience in this human game in this lifetime. It is your infinite self, your Soul Self, who is the creator.

The quickest way to step out of a power struggle with someone is to stop being in a power struggle. Does that mean that you do exactly what they want? No, that's not what that means. It means you just allow them to be the way they are, and you allow yourself to be the way you want to be. You make decisions about how you want to live in this life, and allow them to make their decisions.

Let's say you are in a marriage where you have great benefit from the financial area but not in the emotional area. Some would say that if you stay in a relationship for financial purposes, you are prostituting yourself. What I say is as long as you make a clear decision about what you are doing, it doesn't matter. There is no right or wrong. It is what works for you. It is part of the game. When you roll the dice, it does not matter whether you move to the right or the left. You simply have different experiences depending upon your choice.

What is important is what you believe and feel. You may stay in a relationship with someone who gives you whatever benefits s/he has—be it great wealth, small wealth, or simply security—and no matter what anybody outside of yourself says, if you are comfortable and pleased with where you are, then you are where you need to be.

There is only one person who can decide whether or not to stay in a relationship. That person is you. It does not matter what other people believe; it matters what you believe. It does not matter if someone says you are giving yourself away by wanting something such as financial security—and this can be a metaphor for any kind of security. It does not matter. It matters that you do what is important and comfortable for you. If you are in a relationship that gives you a measure of security but you feel you are being dishonest with yourself, that is where the issue is. If you are perfectly happy and comfortable with such a relationship, then that is fine and it does not matter what anybody else says or believes.

Your power is in doing what you want in the relationship. When you have that feeling of peace and comfort on the inside, you will be right where you need to be. It does not matter what others say and do. You may have plans that you are going to do such and such for a while and then do something different. It doesn't matter what those around you say or think. Some may say that is selfish. Dear Ones, you *are* the center of your universe. Everything in your life revolves around you. Most of you have not been brought up to think that way. But do think about it. Being the center of your universe means *you* make decisions for yourself.

You might say that you have to do certain things because your child needs it. Yes, and at the same time, if you didn't care about your child needing it, you would make a different decision, would you not? So, you are still making the decision based on what you want. Even if you have a variety of reasons why you do things, I'm telling you that you still do those things because of your wants, your desires or your fears. You make the choices based upon what is most important to you.

If you have discomfort about a relationship, when you have (1) accomplished your goals in that relationship, or (2) decided that what you are feeling inside is enough to move you somewhere else, then you will make your decision—even if it's to live under a bridge. Remember, you can do whatever it is you choose to do. Of course, you don't think you can. Because you can't control the other person, relationships are one of the primary ways you convince yourself you are finite and powerless.

Notice now that the encodement technicians are doing some more work with you. The work being done is to assist you in coming to know that you are powerful, infinite beings. It does not matter what happens in the "years" you live upon this Earth in the body you inhabit. When you decide to leave this body behind, when these "clothes" don't serve you anymore, you will leave and you will experience tremendous things you can't imagine right now. You will come to know how everything fits together and who is who. You may even come to know that the one you had the most difficulty with in this incarnation was and is your best friend…and is totally love.

In relationships, whether with a child, a spouse or partner, a friend, a neighbor or whomever, your power is accessed when you take the time to ask, "What is it I would like to have?" You can make a strategic decision about what you would like to do.

In sports, there are plays, are there not? In football, for example, the "X's" and "O's" on the chart show who will do what on each play. It is the same with relationships. What is important is what works for you.

How many of you have heard that tolerance is important? Think about tolerance. Consider the difference between tolerance and acceptance. Isn't there a different energy between tolerance and acceptance? How many of you enjoy being tolerated? Not much, right? Language, as you have created it, is important because there is energy in words. Tolerance implies a different kind of energy than acceptance.

I spoke earlier about how you, an infinite being, set up in this lifetime to experience limitation. In other words, you are playing a game of finiteness, of powerlessness. Since having a relationship with self and with others is part of that game, it serves the perfect purpose of convincing you that you are powerless. By now, you recognize you are moving beyond the "Let's Pretend I'm Limited Game." Every time you do healing in any relationship, you are healing the relationship with yourself. You are removing limitation as you realize, "How can I not have a relationship with self?"

What I would like you to do now is, while in your Heart Source, go into the back of your heart center. I am going to ask those who have passed on from this life who were very important to you, to come to you. I am going to ask them to merge their energies with you so that you can experience that you are not separate. As they merge with you, I merge with you so that you know there is no "me." There is only "I." There is no "you." There is only "I." Thank you, my Dear Ones, for being willing to move deeper into your power.

———·•·———

Relationship with Self

We've gone through several different ways of how you can access power—your own energy system including encodements, the planet, and others. We're going to revisit relationship with self. There is only one central relationship in your life. That is the one with yourself. If that relationship is off-balance, every other relationship in your life will be off-balance. Think about yourself and think about how true that is.

You may have heard people say in a derogatory manner, "Who do you think you are—the center of the universe?" I want you to know the answer to that is "Yes." You *are* the center of your universe. If you are not the center of your universe, there are problems in your relationship with yourself.

When you look outwards, do you look from another's eyes? Do you not look out only from your eyes? When you look out through your eyes and you see the way everything is happening in the universe, you are actually looking at your relationship with everything in the universe, even if it's the person sitting next to you. Everything is based upon your relationship with yourself.

If you feel good about yourself, if you like yourself, if you know that you are Love Incarnate—I mean you *truly* know you are Love Incarnate, your relationship with everyone else will change if it is negative or out-of-balance. Each person brings forth energy from someone with whom they have a relationship. If you are angry and hostile, you will bring out anger and hostility in other people. You bring it out in yourself and you will bring it out in others.

Why? Because you are the center of your universe. Because you are creating other people to reflect back to you what is happening within you.

You know and you have heard it said many times that all is One. You have also heard it said that you are creators of your reality. That means you create the other people in your life. You also create who you want them to be for you. We've touched on that before.

If you are the center of your universe and the creator of your universe, if you love yourself, if you know you are Love Incarnate, you will create people who are loving. Every person is an illusion. You created every person in your world to serve a purpose for you. And you may say, "Wait a minute. I'm reading this because I wished to hear messages from Amma channeled through this person who's known as Cathy." Yes, yet you created this situation to occur so that the words I give through this one are a message you give to yourself, reflecting something back to you or having you move in a different direction.

For those of you who have heard my messages over time, has there ever been a session when you've said, "That doesn't apply to me at all?" Have you ever said, "I feel as though she's speaking directly to me?" You may think on one level that I'm speaking directly to you because I know what it is you need to hear. I am speaking directly to you because you have created this one I'm speaking through to bring me in to give you the words you wish to hear.

In other words, Precious Ones, I am *you* speaking to yourself. If you created me to give you certain words and you find those words filled with great wisdom, who is the wise one? It is *you*. You are the wise one.

We've said that you are an infinite being. Yet everything in this life conspires to deny that reality. You have been learning that you are an infinite being but how many of you truly, truly *know* you are an infinite being? How would you know if you were an infinite being? Think of what an infinite being could be.

An infinite being knows that everything is abundance and would simply breathe in the abundance and breathe out the manifestation of that abundance. Infinite abundance.

An infinite being might have the desire to experience what it would be like to go white water rafting and then create the opportunity to do so. An infinite being might have the desire to experience a relationship with someone who doesn't love him or herself just to see what that play or movie would be like. Some of you may say, "I've got that down pat."

I want you to know you are creating exactly what it is you wish to create and it comes from your relationship with yourself.

Are you ready for another little twist? You may also think you have a "bad" relationship with yourself which is exemplified by your relationships with other people. You may believe this is a flaw within yourself. Dear Ones, you could have decided you wanted to have a part in a play where you would experience being in relationship with someone who did not love you the way you wanted. In fact, that someone would love you the way you love yourself. Think about that.

We have reminded you that some have said you came here to learn certain things. Do you truly believe that? Let me remind you that the concept of you learning something is easy to latch onto to explain upsets and horrors you have experienced. Remember, you did not come to Earth to learn anything. If you are an infinite being, do you need to learn anything? What is true is that you did come here to experience things. Perhaps you came here to experience what it is like to fool yourself and convince yourself that you are not infinite. You set that up pretty well, didn't you?

If you are tired of that creation, how do you go about changing it? Form in your mind right now what it is you want instead. It can be a big thing or a little thing. It can be anything—perfect health, the perfect relationship, financial abundance, abundance of joy. What would you need to do to manifest it?

If you are an infinite being, then you could change that manifestation of what you see in your life. Although I've just said,

"If you are an infinite being...," remember that you *are* an infinite being. Who believes in his or her heart s/he is an infinite being? Who truly believes, to the depths of themselves, that they are Love Incarnate? For those who haven't remembered some of the earlier messages when I use the term "Love Incarnate," is not God's Love all there is? And you were created in the image and likeness of this God? This means you were created in the image and likeness of Love, that you were created from Love. Therefore, you are Love—Love Incarnate.

Believing, not just in your head but in the depths of your heart that you are Love Incarnate, will change everything around you. Will it change what happens in fact? In other words, will believing that you are Love Incarnate change what is happening, for instance, in Iraq? What it will do is change *how you perceive* what is happening in Iraq.

You are Love Incarnate. Every person reading this is Love Incarnate. Every person on this planet is Love Incarnate—and every plant, every animal. You are all made from the same substance. Human beings have a certain way of relating in their Love Incarnate-ness.

If you truly believe you are Love Incarnate and you are the center of your universe, you may choose how you perceive every event, every relationship, every word. If you are interacting with someone and he or she says something you judge to be hurtful, only someone who does not believe they are Love Incarnate would be hurt by the comment. Only someone who believes s/he and the other person are not Love Incarnate could believe the other person would intentionally say something hurtful.

Let me reiterate what I've said earlier. As an infinite being, you are here to experience exactly what you wanted to experience. For example, what would it be like to be in a drama? Life is sometimes a comedy and other times, a melodrama, is it not? I am sure each one of you can list several scenes in your drama. Think about some of the movies you see or some of the comedies on TV. Are not some of the funniest moments in what you call your situation comedies, also some of the most tragic scenes?

Cathy Chapman

I'm going to use this one I speak through as an example. A number of years ago she became very ill with vertigo. She was so ill she had to hold onto her sister in order to go to the bathroom. Holding on to her sister's shoulders, she walked forward with her eyes closed. Her sister was walking backwards. When this one picked up her foot, she couldn't find the floor. Her foot was twirling about trying to locate where the floor was. Someone observing this might have said, "How tragic." But let's put this in another perspective—a situation comedy perspective. Would that not have been hysterical to see someone trying to walk where the foot can't find the floor? Imagine it! The foot is a few inches away from the floor and this person could not find it. What makes the difference between something being sad or funny? The difference is how you perceive it.

I can tell you this one did not think it was very funny at the time. Now she does laugh about it because she imagines what that must have looked like. If this were happening in the context of a 30-minute television show with retorts back and forth, would you not have laughed? It is how you look at it. You have heard it before, do not take yourself so seriously. Finding what can be funny is an example of how not to take yourself too seriously.

You *are* an infinite being. You *are* Love Incarnate.

You have many, many experiences—all of which you have chosen. Some of them look absolutely horrendous—the loss of children, the loss of health, the loss of parents, abuse, jobs disappearing. How many of you have chosen to go to a movie or to watch a television show with those kinds of situations being portrayed? And do you not call that entertainment? Is it entertaining so long as it's not your life?

What is it about the entertainment you have? You know you are watching or are an actor in a play, show or movie that will end in a certain amount of time. You know it is not real. Someone may die from a rare disease and then you see them in another movie or play or show, even the next day. You know the death wasn't real.

If you get in touch with the infinite reality of who you are, you would be able to see your life with the time constraints of a movie, a play or a television show. You would be able to know that this life will end at some point and until then, you could experience all the things you planned.

In this idea of power and relationship with self, what would happen if it really didn't matter what you did? What would you choose to do if it really didn't matter what you chose? Would you choose to rob a bank? Would you choose to have the same players in your play or bring in other players? Walk nude and barefoot on the beach in the moonlight?

Think of some things you would truly enjoy doing. I emphasize the word "enjoy." There is no one reading this who would enjoy robbing a bank and experiencing all the repercussions, is there? If you would truly enjoy doing something, what is keeping you from doing it? Is it because you don't believe you can? You do not have enough faith in yourself? Or is it because you have created others around you to say something like, "Don't be crazy," "Don't be stupid," "Don't be silly"?

You can choose to do whatever you wish. You *are* an infinite being. And yes, you are all, every one of you, One infinite being. You have created every person in your life and every person reading this. You have created everything you see or hear.

You have fashioned the scene in your play. You have set the stage. You decided you wanted to experience your play in one of the largest cities in the United States that is continually under construction. (*This message was first given in Houston, Texas.*) You decided to experience what it was like to dodge cars and traffic. Wouldn't it be fun to be an actor in a play and see what that is like? Think of plays you've participated in when you were little or even in high school. You are an infinite being experiencing this.

Are you saying, "How insane is that?"

Here's the twister. You are the character that your Soul Self, which is you, created to experience this play. Your Soul Self (who you can be in communication with if you wish) is the one who

Cathy Chapman

directs this play. Your Soul Self is the one who knows everything that could possibly happen and may decide at the last minute to change the possibility from one event to another.

The difficulty with where you are now in this physicality, on this planet, is that you feel you are separate from your Soul Self, that you are separate from that infinite part of yourself. Of course, you planned it to be this way. How could you truly experience the play of limitation if you did not lose yourself in the part?

Aren't the best actors and actresses the ones who lose themselves in the part and the viewer forgets who that person really is? When you were acting in that kindergarten, elementary or high school play, or even now if you are acting, aren't your best performances when you lose yourself in the role and forget who you truly are until you take that bow on stage at the end of the play?

You *are* an infinite being. Nothing you can do and nothing that can happen to you on this Earth stage can change that. Is there something that can happen that will convince you that you are not an infinite being? Well, yes, in the play. That happens when you, as an infinite being, decide to come into the world as a tiny baby.

Suddenly an infinite being had to figure out how to use that tiny body. Parents of little ones know well that more food ends up in other places than in the mouth when babies are learning to feed themselves. You think it's cute to show pictures of them covered with spaghetti or oatmeal. That is an infinite being getting used to the limitations of that body. They don't know how to work that little, bitty body.

You had to get used to the nervous system. You know how babies seem to look all around you? The doctors think it's because they can't focus well. The babies are looking at all the colors in your aura. They see the wonderful colors that are changing constantly. Those colors are much more interesting than you are! They remember their infinity more clearly than you do. Sometimes they have absolute frustration while adjusting to the new limitations. You can hear it in their howls.

You still howl, but it is because you have forgotten you are an infinite being. You can't believe you would ever choose something like this life of yours. Your Soul Self is directing this play you are staring in—your Soul Self is *you*. You and your Soul Self are One. But you were "programmed" to forget that "little" detail.

Everyone has guilt about actions or inactions in their life. Your sense of limitation is exacerbated by that guilt. People at times have great sadness or resentment about something done to them. Yet those are nothing more than the experience you wished to have. If you were a character in a play, somebody you chose to be in relationship with rejected you, and everybody believed it including yourself, at the end of the play wouldn't you say that performance deserved a Tony award?

Let's look at Academy Awards. Sometimes the Best Supporting Actor or Actress is not on the movie set for more than five or ten minutes, but that person did an excellent job. What would happen to your life if you, the center of your universe, were able to look at every person as a Best Supporting Actor or Actress? What if you were able to look at every person as Love Incarnate?

What if you were able to look at yourself as Best Actor or Best Actress—that you were playing the part so wonderfully well that you were able to absolutely, totally convince yourself that you were miserable and unlovable and that there was no joy in life? Then the play ended and you stepped off the stage where everything you saw was joy and love and abundance.

Yes, you created all of this. At the same time, the only judgment about what you created is that you did it perfectly. When you have a judgment that says you didn't do it perfectly and you should have done it differently, you are forgetting how well you played the part you wrote for yourself. You will receive your Academy Award when you leave this incarnation. Everyone will greet you and you will greet everyone else and celebrate the good jobs you have done.

There is absolutely nothing you have done from the moment of conception until now, or in other lifetimes, that requires you hold onto shame. Nothing. It does not matter if you chose to have affairs, to rob a bank, to swindle the government, to betray a friend, or to kill someone. It was a part you played. You created yourself to play that part. Others created you to play that part for them. Yes, you might have set yourself up where there are such things as jail, lethal injection or violence. That does not change who you truly are...Love Incarnate.

If you so choose, you can step out of the part of being in an unhappy or unfulfilling relationship. And yes, you can play the part of being a client or patient of some health-care practitioner. You can release the creation of one who sabotages yourself. Your script can be written that way.

What would happen right now if you chose to step out of the guilt, out of the shame, of whatever it is that is holding you back? What would happen? It changes your play. Just look at it as an Academy Award winning performance and say, "Wow. I am so good! I nailed that part to perfection."

In your relationship with yourself, that which keeps you from acknowledging the wonder that you are is your guilt and shame. What I wanted to do in this message is to give you a different way of looking at things—to give you something to think about. It is all in your perspective, in your belief system.

For those who experienced abuse when they were young, what if the belief system was not that the abuse was terrible but the belief system was that the abuse showed love...and you truly believed it? I'm not talking about the perversion of love someone in your script may have said during the abuse. I'm speaking of the being who played that part choosing that role because of unconditional loving support of you and what you wanted to experience.

Is that too much of a stretch for you to believe that it was love? What if you truly believed that, from that particular event, you became a stronger person? People in the military talk about their boot camp experience making them a soldier. It isn't that they enjoyed their boot camp experience but they understand what it did for them. You can release the pain of trauma by looking beneath the experience for what you learned (remembered). This will change the way you look upon things.

What if you looked at a life partner's betrayal as simply a change that provided you with freedom to explore something else in your life? Would that change something in the way you look at what happened? Each event you hold onto, either something done to you or something you did, what if it were simply an experience to give you another tool for later in life? Through such experiences, you are collecting tools to assist in recognizing your creative power. What if you looked at life's experiences in that way?

No one can truly do anything to you. It is all how you created it to be—for a reason, yes. Perhaps the purpose was just to have the experience because you were bored. What I am saying may go against the grain but I want you to look at things a bit differently—to change the way you perceive your life.

I would like now to share some questions previously submitted and answers which may give you more insight.

Q: I can see how the one abused could look at life and say, "I am strong enough to handle this." But what about the abuser? Could you show me how to look at that differently?

A: As the abuser, you may learn to recognize there are certain events that trigger you. You could then experience the accomplishment of self-control. Some people never do learn how to handle the triggers but others do learn.

You may also choose to learn the power of forgiving yourself as well as the one who taught you to abuse.

You can learn about love by having tremendous amounts of love in your life and you can also learn about love by not having love in your life. As the phrase says, there are two sides of the coin. It is the same coin but the sides are very different. There are people who have only abused once. They learned so much about what that did to them (in their movie) that they chose to handle things differently from that point on.

Q: Earth changes have come up a lot in the past year. Do you have any comments on that?

A: Earth changes—yes, there are changes in weather patterns. Some of those are just changes within the natural cycle of weather patterns. Remember that a natural cycle isn't necessarily every ten years. It could be every 10,000 years. What has affected this particular cycle is what governments have done with their experimentation of manipulating the weather. They are trying to make it wet if it's too dry. They are trying to make it warmer or colder. Some of this is just for experimental purposes. Some would call it pure science just to see what would happen. Most governments do it to learn how they can control the weather for military purposes.

Those of you who have been involved with metaphysics for a while know there were supposed to be tremendous Earth changes by now. In fact, the whole world was supposed to be redone by the 1970's, and you're still here.

Remember that any type of information you receive within yourself or from others, like this one who brings me through, is all filtered through that person. Everything is filtered through your own beliefs. One person may read something about Earth changes and it resonates with them and so they bring in more information on the subject.

Let's talk about writing your movie with respect to Earth changes. When you were preparing your script, you selected the various scenes, plots and sub-plots in your life. There are infinite possibilities available to you. This is also true with Earth changes. There are numerous possibilities available. "They" say in California that the "big one" will come soon. "They" said a horrendous hurricane would come, and it came as Katrina. People were expecting this year's hurricane season to be very bad and there was hardly anything. It was like a sneeze. What you call Earth changes may be here. Then again, they may not be coming in the way you expect.

Some things happen not because of Earth changes but because of what you as humans do. Some are from the natural movement of your planet, just as you may look in the mirror and notice something has popped out on your face. It's just a body change, right? If something pops out on the face of the planet, depending upon where it is, the result could be a volcano, a hurricane or even an earthquake.

Q: Is it like a virtual reality video game?

A: Yes, in many ways it is like a virtual reality video game. If it were real, as you were taught, there would be a heaven and a hell and there would be good and bad. There is not. There is only Love. You may ask, "Then why live a certain way?" Well, that makes you happy. When I gave you the question of what you would do if you could do anything, did any of you want to rob a bank? Did any of you want to go tear something apart? Those things do not give joy. That is not how you are made.

You live in this world aware of so much violence. People perform violence from their own perspectives and belief systems. Yours may not be the same as someone living in Iraq or Afghanistan or South Africa or Ecuador or Alaska or Siberia. In fact, you may wonder if you're not coming from different planets if you sat down together and tried to talk about these things.

Yes, it is like a big video game. There is only one ending. You will all finish the video game, leave here, have fun and enjoy each other until your next experience. Right now, you are so immersed in this video game that it feels real to you.

You can play with this world you have created. Those of you in the healing professions, for instance, can create your own healing modalities. You may have a certain modality you learned and know and have worked with, and you can change and create it in any way so that it works better for you.

Those of you who have worked with encodements may remember I have told you:

If you can conceive it, then it can be manifested. It can be done.

Cathy Chapman

Q: I went to a workshop where they told us that we get whatever we really, really, really want or don't want. I'm finding that I'm having a hard time identifying the things that I want. Maybe it's the guilt or the shame or maybe somewhere there's the thought that I don't deserve it. Can you help me with this?

A: One helpful tip is to remind yourself consciously of what it is that you do want. That workshop you went to probably talked about different ways to manifest things. Much of the focusing on what you don't want is habit. It's the not wanting to believe that you are Love Incarnate. There is something in you that says you can't believe that. You were taught that would make you God and you can't be God because there is only one God. That would be blasphemy if you put yourself in that position. What a wonderful way to keep people out of power. Think about that.

You can work with your encodements as you create. Watch and examine what happens each day that moved you toward your goal. Ask to remove, repair or adjust encodements that are moving you where you don't want to go. What did you do which moved you away from your goal? What can you change? It's usually something within yourself.

Try looking at events as if it's an experiment to see what reactions occur. Pretend you are some infinitesimal, finite, ignorant being to see what you can learn from it. Doing this can trigger something deep within you that could move you in a different direction.

Q: Is there a place on Earth that is more conducive to getting outside of the play and seeing the whole picture? Is there a place that supports this?

A: It is only in your head, in your mind, in your heart. It's wherever you choose it to be. Somebody can be in this room and be outside of it, seeing everything as a fun play. They're involved with it, playing different roles, and still know that it is a play. Others are fully immersed in it as a play. If you go to your local store where everybody is shopping and you told them this, what do you think would happen? Would they laugh at you? Lock you up? Yes, perhaps.

Yet some people may have something resonate deep within them even as they laugh at you; "That might be true but then what would I do with everything else? What would I believe?" Where do you fit into what is called a "Christian country" if you believe that you are the center of your universe and are infinite? Where does that fit? It doesn't, does it? So, you feel alone in this perspective. But there are other people like you.

Q: Is there an environment that supports that?

A: It absolutely does not matter what the environment is. You could have a group of people who all believe what I'm sharing with you, yet another person could come in and believe it's all a cult. Even though that one person is surrounded by others who support what you are learning, that other person cannot. It doesn't matter. It is all within you. This is where your power is...within. You can find other people who can give you support.

Q: But that's like a joke.

A: Of course. It is all a joke. Why else would you be told not to take yourself so seriously? Does that rattle some of your belief systems?

You are an infinite being. When you finish this play, this movie, you will go—shall I use the term "Home"? And you will go to the biggest cast party you have ever seen. And that cast party continues and continues as each one of the players finishes his or her role. Think of your play. Have not some of the prime characters already left? They are now at the cast party after having left their bodies. When you leave your body, you will join the cast party.

There is no way that God would deny any creation of God and send it away forever. That does not happen. Everyone is invited to the party. Some will say that if that is so then people can just go ahead and murder and rob and kill. That is an interesting view of life, is it not?

Cathy Chapman

Is it not true, no matter what the belief system, people want to feel important? Why do people strap on bombs and blow up themselves and others? Think about it. What would lead you to do that? You may say "Nothing"—but if that were the only way to save your children or grandchildren, would you do it? And you thought you wouldn't. It's a belief system. If you believed that was the only way to save them, is that what you would do?

You *are* an infinite being—yet you do not believe it. Your infinity has always been present. It's just been hidden. That is how you decided to create it to be.

Religions have been involved in hiding from you the truth that all are saved. How long have your primary religions been in existence? Some, for thousands of years. In many cases, they began with a belief of being able to connect to the Source of All Power. Sometimes they saw the Source of All Power as being a planet or the sun because they felt their power. What you call "pagan" is really a nature religion (Wiccans are an example) where they get in touch with the power that is present in nature.

How do you know which herbs to take? Do you really think somebody accidentally tried an herb and discovered what happened? No. Someone entered into the beingness of that plant or tree and communicated with it. They connected to the consciousness of it. Those of you who can speak to crystals and can hear what they say, or hear what plants or animals say, are connected to that same consciousness. Parents are connected to the consciousness of their infant when they can interpret what different cries mean—"I'm wet," "I'm tired," "I'm hungry." Children, plants, animals—they can all tell you something and you can hear it by entering into their consciousness. At one time, people knew how to do that and they felt in touch with creation.

Then certain belief systems came and convinced people they were "other than." There always seems to be a little power and control involved, or should I say a great deal of power and control. I am not talking about the power that is within you. I'm speaking of the perversion of true power...power over someone. This exercise of power is a separation from the Oneness.

Let's take your Christian tradition. If you discover what were the true words of the man you call Jesus, and you read them in what is called the Christian scriptures, and if you find what is called the apocrypha and read those words, there is much recorded about power.

Imagine how happy you would be right now if you did what is sometimes called forgiveness—forgiveness of everything. Think of the worst thing that has happened to you in your life. If you had an event pop quickly into your mind then it has not been forgiven. If you had forgiven it, you would have let it go and would have a difficult time recalling it. If something immediately popped into your head, you are still holding onto it.

If you are struggling to come up with something, I might ask you if you've lost a parent. "Oh, yes, that was hard." Then I might ask if your parents abused you, if they spanked you, if they left you or anything like that. You might say, "Oh, I remember that now." That means you have forgiven it. You have let it go. You have released it. If you are able to let go of everything that happens, there would not be energy holding you down.

We have talked about being an infinite being and how you decided to play the role of a finite being who has all these things happen, who has an energy field, and more. The only truth is you are an infinite being. The rest is simply illusion. Feeling as if you are a finite being when you are truly infinite is illusion. It feels like paradox.

Now let's do a little meditation. Even this meditation is not truly real. You are still playing a role. It feels good and it's much more fun, for instance, than putting your hand into a pot of boiling water. They are both experiences, are they not?

Be sure you are in your Heart Source.

Now, again enter your heart center from the front. Go deep within your heart center. At the same time go into your heart center from the back. Go deep within from the back of your heart center. Go deeply there.

You will come to your sacred space. Go even more deeply until you come face-to-face with yourself. Look at yourself eye to eye. Look deeply within your soul.

Enter into the infinity of yourself. Look into your eyes and say to the other aspect of yourself, "You are Love Incarnate." There are two aspects of yourself saying, "You are Love Incarnate."

Now say, "I am Love Incarnate."

Surrounding you are all those you call angels, guides, encodement technicians, family members who have gone before you, and family members yet to come. They gather around you and hold you in the love emanating from their hearts. As a group, in one voice—maybe in harmony, they say, "*You* are Love Incarnate. You are perfect exactly as you are. *You* are Love Incarnate."

With all this love surrounding you, with all the reminders of who you are, take that one thing you recalled—the worst thing that happened to you—and see, feel, experience the energy of pain from that event fall away from you. Just let it fall out of you—out your feet, your pores, or however you wish to image it.

You can do this exercise at any time. Be in the midst of all this love and choose to let go of your judgment about something. Then what is left is love, joy, the essence of who you truly are— Love Incarnate.

Now, Dear Ones, I hold my hands upon you and send my love into you. This is not a love you need because you are already *love*. That is simply who you are. The love I send to you is *who you are.* My blessings to you. I am Amma, the Divine Mother. We are truly one and we are truly Love.

———•·•———

Increasing Your Experience of Power

*A*uthor's Note: This message was given in Arizona to a group who asked Amma how they could increase their personal power. It is a good review of her teachings with some new insights. I've edited this information to incorporate the Heart Source. —Cathy

---

The Heart Source

You form the Heart Source through the following steps:

1. Enter into the back of your heart center.
2. Enter into the front of your heart center.
3. Enter into the front of your brow center.
4. Enter into the back of your brow center.
5. Connect your heart center with your brow center with a beam of light moving through your pranic tube from the heart center to the brow.
6. Move that beam of light up to the Center of the Universe (don't worry where that is).
7. Move the light to the center of the earth.

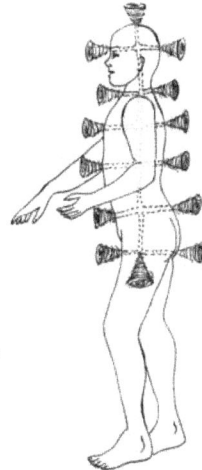

Good evening, Dear Ones. How wonderful to be here with you in this grand place. This is a high energy location. We have the honor of being in an area where a vortex is forming. This is not a vortex as some would explain using ley lines. This is a particular energy system that is forming to surround this area. It will actually encompass your entire downtown area of Winslow, Arizona. It will be a wonderful place. There will be many changes coming for this area. It will become known as a spiritual center in many ways. Those of you here are going to be part of this expansion in the various ways you experience your spirituality. I honor you for that. Those of you who came from other states to live here, came for this spiritual purpose. It will be great fun as long as you ignore all the naysayers. Yes, it will be great fun.

I am Amma. I am the Divine Mother of the divine mothers, and I am your mother. Did you catch the logic of that? You also are divine. We have divine mothers and divine fathers here in this room. All of you reading these words are divine mothers and divine fathers. Think of the meaning of the words "mother" and "father." They are nurturers. They are life-givers. They are guides. They are mentors. Anyone who has not accepted those roles has not accepted their divinity. Think about that. Whether or not you have physical children, you are, in your divinity, a mother or a father as you are to be a teacher—one who guides and teaches—one who loves those around you.

I am not talking about standing on street corners and preaching. I am talking about standing in line at the bank, the airport, the post office, or waiting for a traffic light. I am talking about casting your divinity outward by being in your Heart Source and radiating the love that you are to other people.

My Dear Ones, remember that you are nothing less than Love Incarnate. *Nothing less than Love Incarnate.* This love is not the emotion you read about, hear in songs, or see in the movies. The love I'm referring to is used by those who do the heroic thing of being true to themselves and true to another. That is when you are most expressing yourself as Love Incarnate. You are living love when you come forth and be who you truly are. That is when you are in your power.

Look at those around you in this room. They are aspects of yourself as they are also Love Incarnate. They are created from the same energy I call love. You may wonder where those wondrous thoughts or words come from which sometimes come through you. They come from the very love from which you are made. Every one of you is made from that love. Every person you revere as a great master, teacher or leader is made from the same love from which you were created.

You each have the love energy you can access. You are right now, at this very moment, connected to that energy. You have the ability to get any information you want or need. If you need those words of wisdom, you can go into that deep place within yourself and ask. By setting your intention to connect to love, the energy will come through you. Yes, you will be channeling—channeling that energy as this one does. She interprets the energy in her way through her energy, through her belief system. And you will do the same thing. The same energy can come through each of you simultaneously. You may each use different words, different expressions, to interpret the information, but it will be from the same energy. That is the wonder of this spiritual expansion. Each one of you bringing through the same energy will give a different perspective on a situation, and together you will have a whole.

I wish to emphasize—you are divinity. You are Love Incarnate. And every person you see is the same, no matter how heinous or saintly he or she may be. You are all made of the same "stuff."

Let's talk about your own power, your own Love Incarnate-ness, your own divinity. I'm going to express and explain different ways you can tap into the energy of love so you can cope with the repercussions of those who don't know they are divine and are Love Incarnate. That is what you are facing, is it not, in this world as it changes?

Everyone is Love Incarnate. Everyone is divine. Not everyone remembers this. No one here or reading this knows it to the depths of their hearts. But you know the idea, do you not? You are familiar with the idea that you are infinite, spiritual beings who came to this planet for this human experience. You came here for the experience of limitation. You may ask why you would do that. I will answer as any three year old would answer: Because.

Because you wanted the experience. You cannot understand, in your trials and your troubles, why you would want to experience such things. Why would anyone want to experience grief, addiction or not believing who he or she is? Why would anyone have to experience that? Yes, that is what a limited being would ask—one who is not aware of infinity.

I'm going to ask you to let go of attempting to figure this out. You cannot figure it out. You can come up with all kinds of reasons and rationalizations for anything. The truth, no matter how much you wish to battle it, is that you chose to experience this. Yes, you chose it. Do the words, "Thy will be done" sound familiar? Let me say that, in this case, it is *your* will be done. You will argue and say it is not your will.

Let's talk about your Soul Self. Your Soul Self is the you who knows it is infinite. It is that aspect of you who does not forget. It is that aspect of you who directs the infant who couldn't even roll over or feed him or herself. You, as your Soul Self, went to great lengths to convince yourself, your persona, to forget that you are infinite. So, "Thy will be done" is knowing that your Soul Self is in charge of the entire plan of your life and is working with you on a soul level. The least you resist it, the easier it will be.

Things are difficult, right? You do not like to bring difficult things to mind. Dear Ones, things are going to become more difficult. You are having difficulties here in your country, the United States, with your economy. You are going to have difficulties in your political scene even though you may think it couldn't be any worse with the current division between the right and the left, the conservative and the liberal. Yes, things are already beginning to "juice up," you might say. Unfortunately, for those in your highest political office, you see racism rear its head again. You will see a backlash against women again—the difference between aggressive and assertive. You will see all of this. It will occur. Great divisions are happening.

I'm going to present a paradox. It may seem strange to you that I would say this: *Take no side but know where you stand.*

Let's talk about taking no side. Accept people where they are. Take no side. Do not try to make anyone into someone else. If someone comes to you and tells you that what you believe is an affront to God because you can only believe in a Christian God or an Islamic God or a Jewish God or whatever, accept that that is where they are—*and you know where you are.* Do not try to change them. There is no reason to do that. They are revealing to you that part of yourself that is so terrified of uncertainty and anything that is not black and white. They are revealing where you are so terrified of accepting your own responsibility for how you live your life, of being terrified of living in your power.

I am going to give you some suggestions on how to live your life. Simultaneously, I'm going to tell you that if you choose to live life differently, I will love you and hold you in the highest regard. That is different from what others teach, is it not? It does not matter to me what you believe, what you feel, or what you experience. Do you know why? *I know who you are. Yes, I know who you are. You are Love Incarnate. You came from my womb.* I know all of your lifetimes. I even know how the decisions you are making in this lifetime are affecting your future lifetimes and your past lifetimes, both of which you are living right now. There is no time, is there?

You have heard it said that there is nothing impossible for God. Yes, there is. It is impossible for me to *not* love you. It is impossible for me to *not* know who you are. It is impossible. I ask you to examine and think about whether or not you can believe that. If you can believe what I have just said, then you can be accepting of others.

When I say, "Know where you stand," some may think that means to know which side you are on. No, I mean *know where you stand.* Remain firm in your own beliefs. Do not allow someone else to talk you out of what you believe. Take what they say and evaluate it in a dialectic manner. For example, what if I tell you that all of you here must live on a cruise ship in the Atlantic? Yes, some of you may think that would be very nice. To evaluate that in a dialectic way, look at every argument for and every argument against living on a cruise ship in the Atlantic. You would then know as much as possible and could decide where you stand on that suggestion.

Do not discard out of hand someone's belief about who God is unless you have thought about it, considered it, evaluated it, and gone into your heart to discover what is true for you. That is what I mean by "take no side but know where you stand."

There is much going on between your traditional, conservative Christianity here in the United States and others who wish to believe contrary to Christianity. You will notice that in a deep spiritual tradition—not a deep religious tradition but a deep spiritual tradition—all will come to the place within their hearts of union with themselves, with each other, with the Earth, with the sky, and with what some call God. This is where your power lies—in the Oneness.

I challenge you to examine this for yourself. Know what you believe. Know where you stand. It is only by knowing where you stand that you will prevent yourself from being buffeted from side to side. Knowing where you stand means you will be deeply rooted where you are. You will not be like a tree with shallow roots and be blown over. It does not matter where you stand. It only matters that you *know where you stand.*

As the spiritual vibration on this planet rises, it is imperative that you know where you stand because those who do not, and who are terrified of something different, are going to express anger, bitterness, accusation and so on. This is because of their fear. It is because of them, not because of you. They see in you a reflection of that part of themselves they don't want to believe they are, and are so afraid. I hope this is making sense to you. Remember—know where you stand.

If you are in a relationship in which you are unhappy, make a change and take a different stand. If you are in a job, profession, city, family—find out where you stand. If you are standing in the wrong place for you, make changes. Move to where you know you can stand. Know where you stand.

It is time for people on this planet to quit letting others think for them. Each person can choose whatever political party he or she wishes, whatever side or spectrum, whichever religious or spiritual tradition he or she wishes. It does not matter. You make your choice because you want to do it—because you believe in your choice. It does not matter in this country if you vote Democrat or Republican. What matters is if you do it because that is what you believe and not because someone else tells you to do so.

When you finish this lifetime you will review your life. You will measure yourself in the success of what you wanted to accomplish, by how much you did, acted, reacted, expressed (use whatever words you wish) of what you believed and knew was true. Every person comes here to experience something different, and people join together in their experiences. You will then discover there was nothing to measure. It was all perfect.

I would like to summarize some of what I have talked about over the past few years. I'm going to give you some tools. These tools are for those who know where they stand. They are tools you can use. The very first tool is to be in your Heart Source. I say that no matter who I come through, and I come through more than this one. *Be in your Heart Source or, at the very least, in your heart.*

Those who do not know or believe there are chakras or energy centers, do know they have a physical heart. Those of you who know my work will remember that the physical heart has its own energy structure that works with the entire physical body. There is a close connection between your heart center and your physical heart. If you focus on one, the other is activated. I challenge you to learn to live your life from this place, from your heart.

I often invite you to go into your heart center through the back of your heart chakra. In the back of your heart chakra, you have an entryway into inter-dimensionality. Entering through the front of your heart leads you to experiences mostly of this incarnation. When you go into your heart chakra from the back, into your sacred space—to your altar as I have called it—you can connect to a variety of exciting information, energies and people. You can go into other lifetimes—past, present and future. You can travel to other planets. You can experience many wondrous things.

Going into the front of your heart chakra, you are more contained in this physicality. Yes, people do go into the front of their heart chakra and up their pranic tube and travel from there. But try it through the back. It's easier.

After you have become used to staying within your heart center, you might want to work on experiencing being in the front and the back of the heart center at the same time. (Those of you familiar with the Heart Source, recognize this step.) Try it right now.

Go into your heart from the front.... Now, with a little bi-location, stay there and go into your heart center from the back.... Experience the difference.... Can you feel the difference?

Here is a suggested plan of action. Make a commitment for one week to spend time in your heart by going in through the front of your heart center. Do something to remind yourself. Put post-it notes everywhere. You might wonder if you can think as easily if you're in your heart center and not in your mind. Dear Ones, be in your heart center and extend the energy to connect all the chakras to your heart center. You are living fully from your heart. You live, for example, in your first chakra and from your heart, from your second chakra and from your heart, from your third chakra and from your heart, from your throat chakra and from your heart, from your third eye and from your heart, and from your crown as well as your heart. It's always from your heart.

When an infant is born, almost always the first chakra is open. If it is not, the infant is sick and may be struggling to decide whether or not to stay in this lifetime. All the other chakras, except the crown, are closed. This is part of the process of forgetting your infinity. You come in as a little infant with the first chakra open so you can stay in this lifetime. And the crown is open as it is the only connection to who you truly are. The other chakras are not open. As the child learns and grows the other chakras begin to open.

You will find with today's children that their heart chakras opened much earlier than yours. In fact, some of these children are now coming in with their chakras already open. You know them— these little ones who come out with words of great wisdom that you listen in wonder. They display a large amount of unconditional love, that energy which flows outwards without any expectation of it being returned.

You need to learn how to activate each of your chakras in union with your heart. When, for instance, you are at work or anywhere else that you have to solve a problem, go into your heart first and then bring the energies up into your head. When you are getting ready to make love, go into your heart first and then bring your energies into your second chakra. When you go out to give a talk, go into your heart then move the energies to the third and fifth chakras, the solar plexus and throat. Learn to activate all the chakras.

Take it one step at a time. During the first week, just practice going into the front of your heart center. The next week, stay in the front of your heart chakra *and* move into the back of your heart chakra. You will discover, as you stay in this space, you will have different experiences. You will find you are aware of more. Stick with this exercise. If you make this your focus, you will discover that amazing things happen. You will find your intuition expanding. You will discover you have access to inter-dimensional energy if you live while being in both the front and the back of your heart center.

Now, while in your Heart Source, begin to focus outward. When you are greeting someone, say to yourself, "You are Love Incarnate. I, as Love Incarnate, greet you as Love Incarnate." In this way, you set the energy for relating to another Love Incarnate. Even if this is someone with whom you have an uneasy relationship, you will be soothing the energy between you.

Let's say your boss is yelling at you. When you stay in your Heart Source and say to yourself, "You are Love Incarnate," the hostile energy from the yelling boss cannot penetrate your energy.

This is what some call psychic protection. There is no way that low vibration energy can penetrate the energy of your Heart Source when you are proclaiming the truth, "I am Love Incarnate and you are Love Incarnate."

If you are reading the newspaper or watching the news, and you feel the emotion of fear or anger, that is your signal that you are not in your Heart Source. Go back into your Heart Source. Declare the truth, "I am Love Incarnate and you are Love Incarnate."

Simple, is it not? Easy? No, it is not. This is a discipline. Isn't it amazing that you have to have a discipline so you can come to know who you truly are? That is what this exercise is for—to come to know who you truly are, to come into your power. You will find, as you relate to anyone in this way, be it in print, on television or in person, energy will begin to shift in relationship with the other. This is because, as you increase your experience of who you are, you increase the energy coming into your Heart Source resulting in continual expansion. Your love energy emanates outwards to others.

Do you know what happens when it emanates outwards? The other is faced with a choice: "Do I accept this energy or do I reject it?" It is their choice—totally theirs. They are mirroring to you the choice you have every day, in every way: Do I accept who I am or do I reject who I am? Everything you do, every thought you make, every choice presented to you asks: Is this who I am or is this a rejection of who I am?

You are conditioned to believe you are anything but Love Incarnate. You have been conditioned to believe that if you claim you are Love Incarnate, that it is blasphemy—even evil itself is speaking. When someone says to you, "Who do you think you are—the center of the universe? Do you think you're God ?" You go into shame as the question was intended for you to do. The answer, of course, is "Yes, I am." The more you act upon this truth, the more you believe this truth, the more events and cellular memories come to mind to reinforce you are not Love Incarnate. In the game of limitation you are not meant to know you are precious beyond words.

You will benefit greatly if you work with your encodements. Here's a brief review. Let's say you have a memory come up that hurts or moves you into fear. When that happens, talk to your encodement technicians. Remember that you contact your encodement technicians by being in your Heart Source and going into the back of your heart center. Once you have become adept at working with your encodement technicians, they are available to speak with at any time. They are aspects of you.

Ask your encodement technicians if there are any artificial encodements holding in the energy of the pain or fear you feel at the memory of this event. You will receive a "yes". If there were not any artificial encodements, that feeling would not come up.

Then ask what the consequences would be of removing these artificial encodements. I always suggest to those just learning the encodement process to ask about consequences. This gives you the opportunity to accept the change or not. There can be any number of changes ranging from almost nothing at all, to absolute fear, to being sick for a week. Those who have done encodement work for a while and are used to the consequences, don't even go to that question. They just request that it be done. They will say, "Remove the artificial encodements."

The next question is if there are any natural encodements that were damaged or altered as a result of the event. Do ask what the consequences would be if these are repaired. For example, someone you loved dearly has passed on and, years later, you are still in extreme grief. The natural encodements connecting you to that one no longer need to be active. If they are active, you can ask that they be deactivated. A different way of handling grief, is it not? This can be done when you feel the grief you carry is debilitating. If the consequences are agreeable to you, ask that these natural encodements be deactivated. Then take a deep breath and give this process a chance to work. It may take a few days. Your love for the other will never go away, but the pain will be greatly decreased or eliminated.

We'll experiment with this now. I want you to think of an event that occurred recently and brought up something in your past. Do you have something in mind?

Staying in your Heart Source, ask for your encodement technicians to come. You may see, feel or sense your encodement technicians. Most of you have three of them. Some of you have three plus one or two apprentices who have come with their teacher to observe.

Ask if there are any artificial encodements holding the pain of this event in your system. Ask what the consequences would be if these were removed. Even if you know you will have them removed, you may want to know the consequences. If you are willing to accept the consequences, ask that those artificial encodements be removed or deactivated. You don't have to know which; the encodement technicians know what to do.

Now ask if there are any natural encodements damaged or altered that hold in the pain from this event. Ask what the consequences would be of having them repaired. If you are agreeable to the consequences, ask that it be done.

Some of you will immediately experience a difference. I would like you again to bring that memory to mind. Notice if it feels any different. Does it have the same charge? If it still feels the same, give yourself some time. Some of you are feeling a difference now. Is it that easy? Yes, it can be that easy.

Use this in any way your imagination leads you. If you ever question whether or not you can use encodement work for something, know that the answer is "yes." You may need to experiment with it in different ways. Sometimes you may need to do encodement work in conjunction with some other healing. Any who work as healers can do encodement work with others. You can do it even if your clients do not know you are doing it. Since they have come to you for healing you do not need to ask further permission. You can communicate with their encodement technicians and ask if it is permissible to work with them. Encodement work is always occurring when healing is in progress. The encodement technicians are always working with the energy of the one who has come to you. When you ask, it happens more quickly.

Are there any questions?

Q: Could you mention that technique you've talked about before about going in and helping another person by inserting all the love in their hearts?

A: Why don't you talk about how that worked for you?

Q: Well, I feel it's made a difference. I do it all the time with my kids and my grandchildren. It's about going into the back of your heart, going to your altar—however you picture your altar. You see yourself walking into this white pillar of light. Staying in this white pillar of light, picture the person you are praying for. Go into the back of their heart and send them all the love they didn't get that day. Fill them up with love. Then ask Michael, the archangel, to please put his sword of healing into their aura. His sword can be as large or as small as needed. It can go anywhere. I think this really helps. If you have very trying or worrisome situations where you feel you can't do anything and you care so much about these people, this is a great exercise.

A: Thank you. Did you all get how to do that? It is very simple, is it not? And it is very powerful. If you have children or others at home, you can place your hand upon them at night (physically or in the etheric) and ask that they receive all the love they needed or wanted that day and didn't receive.

Here is another tool. Bring to mind that wound or event you brought up earlier. While in your Heart Source, go into the back of your heart center. See the event where you received that wound. Go into the pillar of light, which is the light that comes through you. Send to yourself all the love you needed then but did not receive. You can also do this for yourself when you were growing in the womb. Powerful, isn't it?

The more you do this, the more you know yourself as Love. You come to know who you are as Love—the power that you are as

Love. It brings back the knowledge of your worthiness. So much happens to you as humans that your sense of worthiness has been eroded and even blasted away. Now you can re-member and know yourself as Love—as Love Incarnate.

You can use this tool if you are dealing with any kind of addiction, be it food or shopping or a chemical of some kind. Do you know what addiction is? It's that feeling of requiring something external to yourself to avoid realizing you don't know who you are. Anyone who does not have an addiction has no idea of its power. Addiction is one of the greatest powers debilitating you when you have it. People die of addiction. Even though they want to live, they can't stop the addiction.

What can be done? You can do encodement work on it. You can ask your encodement technicians to go back to the very first wound that occurred which set up the addiction. It could have begun in the womb. Some will say addiction is genetic. Yes, that is true but the gene is not triggered immediately. Something has to happen. You can do encodement work on the event. And you can go into the back of your heart center, as we just did, and send love to yourself at that time—and continue to do it. You will see changes occur.

Sometimes you will feel as though you are battling with yourself. For those of you who have addictions, is it not true, that at times, you want only to forget what is going on in your life. You can assist those struggling with addiction by communicating with them on a soul level and sending them love. Surround them with love and send them all the love they needed but didn't receive.

Many addicts become stuck on this Earth plane at their death. That is what makes it more painful. If you know of addicts who have passed on, perhaps they haven't made it back to the Light. You know the Archangel Mich-a-el also known as Michael. He is usually pictured with the sword in his hand. He will give you his sword. All you need to do is to ask for it.

Go into the back of your heart center right now. Call upon Mich-a-el, the Archangel. Some of you call him St. Michael. Ask him for the use of his sword. He will place it in your dominant hand. Simply open your hand. You can do it physically or do it in your mind's eye. Feel the sword in your hand. This sword can become as large as necessary, miles long or even spanning universes, or as small as needed to where it could go into the DNA. You can use it to destroy thought forms. You can use it to sever attachments.

Think of someone you know who is in pain of some kind—anger, fear, grief. All of that energy will be in their aura. Go with the sword and ask to place it within the energy around that person. Feel, see or sense what happens.

You can use this sword on a country. If any of you have someone fighting in a country whether it be Iraq, Afghanistan, even the Texas or Arizona border, ask to be taken to the location where there is a great deal of negative energy. Know that you are bi-locating to the place. Sense the congested energy and put the sword into the congestion. It will transmute the negativity.

With yourself, do you have a pain in your stomach, your shoulder or anxiety? Just ask to be guided where to place the tip of the sword. Feel, see or sense what happens.

Now hold the sword in front of you. Expand your Heart Source—expand, expand and expand. Have the energy go from your heart into your shoulder and out the sword. See or feel the sword glowing and feel or sense its energy surrounding you. This is another means of what you call psychic protection. It will strengthen your energy field. Those times when you feel you are not in your heart, when you've become caught in the belief that you are less than what you are, use the sword. When you are in fear or anxiety and that low vibration energy is swirling around you, use the sword. It is always available. Call it forth and circle it around you to remove the negative energy.

If you know you are going to walk into a difficult situation put the sword in front of you. You can use it as the anger or low vibration thought forms come at you. Stay in your Heart Source while you do this. Know that you are Love Incarnate and that the other is Love Incarnate. Unfortunately, the other one doesn't remember who he or she is.

I would now like to talk about working with your physical body. I mentioned earlier the properties in the physical heart. Focus on your physical heart right now. Go to the top sixth of your physical heart. You can easily divide the heart into three horizontal planes, and then divide the top plane into halves. That top part, the top sixth of your physical heart, and an equal distance above it, comprise an energy center. Focus on it. Get in touch with it. Go back and forth between your heart chakra and that energy center. Feel the difference. That area in your physical heart can balance your physical body.

Dear Ones, your physical heart is the "brain" of your physical body. The controlling factor in your physical body is your physical heart and the energy center there.

Pick a part of your body that is out of balance. It could be an organ, body part or endocrine gland, even a system such as circulatory or digestive system. Each one of those has its own soul or consciousness. Focus on the energy center of your physical heart. Bring to mind the other part of your body and feel the energy there. As you connect with these two energies, you come into balance. Feel that happening. You need do nothing more than that. Feel the difference?

These tools I have given you are for you to use. You will find your life flowing more easily if you experiment with using them. Discover which ones work best for you. You are coming into your power as you do this.

Are there any other questions?

Q: I would like to ask specifically about my situation of working with children who are sad and angry and hurt. I'm pretty clear that the reason they express themselves as being angry is because that's the only emotion they feel where they have any power. I can see where I can apply these techniques in my work. But I wanted to ask if there might be another technique for me to use to connect with them.

A: What you are doing is wonderful. You've seen changes, have you not? Do you have an office, a place where they come?

(*Yes.*) Ask that a pillar of light be established in the center of that space and expand outward to enclose the entire area. Then ask that love totally enclose it as if you were in a sphere. You have already been doing this, but this process is a more conscious creating of sacred space. You can do this anywhere. This process will help you stay in tune with, and in touch with, who you are. Their anger attempts to convince you they are other than who they truly are.

You are right in that the most power they feel is in their anger. Notice that some express their anger outwardly and some hold it within. Although those who express their anger outwardly are the ones others fear the most, the ones who pull their anger inward are those most likely to do the greatest damage to themselves. When you have this pillar of light in your space, as well as within you, it can neutralize some of this anger.

Continue doing the encodement work with them, as you have been doing. Each time you touch them, even if you cannot do it physically, send energy from your heart to them and ask that they receive all the love they need. When you are sending energy from your heart, you are in your Heart Source with the energy coming from above and below, and going out from your heart. If you are not connected in this way, you will find yourself being depleted. Does that help? (*Yes; thank you.*)

Q: When you talked about the top sixth of the heart, what does the other part represent?

A: The other is just the physical part. There are neural (brain) energies and actual neural tissue going into the bottom part of the physical heart. Every organ has its own soul, or consciousness. You are accessing the soul of the physical heart when you take the top sixth and an equal distance above the heart. Together they equal about one-third the size of the physical heart. If someone has heart disease and the heart is enlarged, this energy center does not enlarge. It remains the same size it would be with a healthy heart.

Focus right now on your liver. Get a connection with your liver. Now connect it with that top part of your physical heart. People continually need their liver cleared, and you can ask for it to be done. If you connect the soul of the liver with the soul of the spleen, for instance, they will have a connection but there will not be the same response as connecting with the energy center of the heart. By connecting a part of the body to the top sixth of the heart, that part of the heart actually brings into balance the other body part, the liver in this case. It brings it into balance and union with the rest of the body.

Q: *To repair damage in the liver, is the most effective way to work with the heart or to work with encodements?*

A: The answer is both. You can work with the energy center in the heart and the liver. If you work with encodements at the same time, it will progress faster. Remember that the liver holds onto anger. Its primary focus is to bring the anger away from the fragile organs in your body. You can ask the encodement technicians if there are any artificial encodements holding onto anger; if so, ask they be released. If you work with that part of your heart and your liver, it can facilitate the clearing much more quickly.

It also works quicker if you are not putting as much garbage into your body. It is very difficult because you breathe in some of that garbage no matter where you are. Just know that the cleansing can occur. If you keep yourself clear of low vibration energies, it almost doesn't matter what you put into your body through your nose or your mouth. When anger is in the liver, it compounds damage from other substances.

Q: *I come from a land that is pretty much void of people. Many of the young ones, including my relatives, have been relocated. A law was passed by the Congress saying we had to relocate and that caused a lot of sadness among my people. Is there any kind of recourse we could work on to bring the land back to my people?*

A: I'm going to address two different issues. The first is regarding the sadness. My comments don't have to do with the changing or relocation. They have to do with the sadness. You can work with the artificial encodements that have come about because of the sadness. You have a very difficult decision to make. Do you want the encodements deactivated that bond you to the land you were relocated from? This is where it gets complex. Do you want to be back with that land, or do you want to release the sadness and be on the other land?

The problem is that your people—and others who had been here for so long—have a bonding with the land that identifies who they are, which most other peoples do not have. This bonding with the land is something that occurs after centuries and centuries of being on the same land and being in communion with that land.

With regard to the sadness, one of the things that can help your people is to work with Michael's sword in removing the energy of the sadness that is there. You can also ask that the artificial encodements, exhibited in many of your people as despair, be removed. You do know, do you not, that much of the energy of despair and hopelessness that your people suffer from is the result of a curse? It was signed into law. In order for you to find who you are, the energy of that curse needs to be broken. You will know how to do that through your own ceremonies and by teaching your young ones so they can know who they are as tribal members. The work many are doing in trying to bring the memories back to your young ones is being diminished because of the curse that comes from that law.

You need to build an energetic wall around yourselves. As I was speaking to the other one about bringing a pillar of light into her office, you can do the same. There needs to be a group of you who come together and bring forth a pillar of light onto the land from which you were evicted. It needs to be nourished by your love, not by your sadness. Your sadness has become debilitating. The sadness and despair have to be dispelled first. You have to find a way to bring the light energy around you. Your people already have ways to do this.

Bring the energy around you so that it neutralizes the energy that came about because of the law. You are not going to find very many people, outside of your people, who care. That is the greatest sadness, is it not? You are a stranger in your own land. People do not recognize that you are bound to this land. That is one of the problems, by the way, of the land itself. It feels that disconnection. There is no one there to nourish it anymore. All those who live on it now, and have no connection to it, will suffer the effects of that disconnection. You and your people are suffering the effects of the disconnection in your spirit. Your people who still hold to your ways have the knowledge and the ceremonies to break the energy. You know that this is your land.

The deep sorrow you and your people carry has gone into the very substance of the land. The land has absorbed your horror. It cries out in anger and fear. As much as these others have denied what that is, they have denied who they are. They don't want you to know who you are. You must find out how to change this from within yourself because they will not help you. They don't want to help you. They are afraid that, if they do, then they will lose the land they have taken.

Dear Ones, I think you now know the depth of pain this one and his people are carrying. Some of you have moved out of your heart because it was too hard to be there. You felt his pain and the pain of his people. You forget that you are One. And you know that you, in the form of your government, has been instrumental in creating that separateness.

Go, now, back into your heart. That is where your power lies. With every situation your life brings you, I remind you to *know where you stand.*

I am Amma, your mother and the Divine Mother of the divine mothers. Remember that you grew in my womb. I am always yours—and you are always mine.

Cathy Chapman

Remembering Who You Are

Let's talk about what you have learned. As an incarnated infinite being playing the game of limitation, you have decided to experience Who You Truly Are. That's the awakening that has been talked about for several decades. There are many of you who have decided to experience this awakening. Many reading these words have already been experiencing you as powerful beings. Some of you have spoken about how you're having more fun in life—how it's exciting for you. You are re-membering who you are and the infinite power you possess.

You may say, "What about 2012 and the shift that is supposed to occur? Does this negate all I've experienced?" No, of course not. It does not negate anything. It is all part of how things are developing in your world, like jigsaw pieces coming together.

I'm sure you have noticed that some people seem to attract particular kinds of events and people; then they change the way they think and they begin to attract something different. You can change what you attract in an instant. *You,* your Soul Self and your persona—together they are Y*ou.* And you have set up this wonderful experience in which you let things unfold gradually. You created your own experience here. You created it before you incarnated. You have heard about everyone gathering together and identified which role they would play in your play. Yes, you did that. Each one of you created your own experience.

Think about the difficulties you have overcome. What has it been like for you to overcome those things? Recall those times when you were suddenly aware of the things you could do—the power that you had. You were re-membering Who You Truly Are.

Become the Love That You Are. You are Love Incarnate. *Become the love that you are.* It might be better to say: *Remember the love that you are.* With each awareness of the high vibration energy entering the planet, you *are* re-membering who you are. This is not something that is easy to grasp. It is not something you can understand with your human mind of limitation.

What can you do to speed this process? It's obvious you want to re-member *who you truly are.* We've talked a great deal about encodement work. I'd like to focus on encodements again as related to your power.

Every person reading these words knows what their body likes to eat and not eat. Even as I speak, it goes through your mind, am I right? Is there anybody who does not know what chocolate cake does to his or her system? Or ice cream? Or candy? I'm not only talking about the negative aspects. Think of the last dessert you had that was exquisite. Wasn't it fun? I want to point out that you have accepted a collective belief system that some experiences were not good for you. Have you noticed in this country of the United States of America that the more focus there is on what you should not eat, the greater the obesity rate, the higher the incidences of heart problems. Have you noticed that?

You created, all of you together, these beliefs about food. Some call the energy of these beliefs a morphogenic field; some refer to it as the matrix. Your creation of this energy about food, this morphogenic field, is a demonstration of how powerful you are. You are amazing creators because you have created these fantasic beliefs about food.

What would happen if I brought in your favorite dessert right now? You realize, of course, each of you would see your favorite. And you were offered an opportunity to partake of that delicious dessert and enjoy it to the fullest. How many of you would be reluctant to have some because of what it would do to your body? Or because of the guilt—"Oh, I shouldn't"?

You have created a body that responds in particular ways to foods and substances. As long as you are in the creation of that body, your body will respond as you have accepted beliefs from other people. The first time you had your favorite dessert, did anybody tell you it was bad for you? No, of course not. But then somebody did. And then the guilt came. You have created this web or matrix of energy of beliefs and that energy of guilt continues to come...and come. So, all you have to do is to look at chocolate cake and you gain ten pounds.

You are infinite beings. You have infinite power. You are ones who can create infinitely. You chose to come to this planet and experience limitation and to believe you cannot create life differently. Now you are remembering you have the power to change your current creations. To manifest new creations, you must first disconnect yourself from the beliefs of others. How can you be your own person if you accept the beliefs of others? Think about it.

How many of you have left a church because you chose not to believe certain teachings anymore? How many of you have left a group of people because you chose not to align with their beliefs any longer? How many of you have left families because you have chosen not to agree with their beliefs of how they treat people?

You made choices to leave certain groups. Is your life different now? Is it extremely different? Can you imagine where you would be now if you hadn't made those changes? This one I'm speaking through said, "Dead." Yes, it may not be physically dead, but you can be dead emotionally with bitterness and anger. You used your power, your wisdom, to make the choice to dramatically change your life by choosing to end your connection with certain beliefs. You made these changes because you were in great pain. It took great pain to move you to the junction of leaving.

Dear Ones, you don't have to experience such pain to "force" yourself to choose new beliefs. You do not have to go through great pain to choose to create something different for yourself. You can choose to change simply because you have the desire to do so. You can, for instance, choose to fully enjoy your favorite dessert. But how can you if guilt is there? Let's do a little exercise.

Imagine your favorite dessert or favorite food you feel guilty about eating…even though you are enjoying it somewhat. Imagine the taste of the food. Feel the guilt that interferes with your enjoyment. I want you to say to yourself: "I disassociate myself, disconnect myself, cut myself off from all the guilt I have accepted from other people with regard to this dessert or food." Ask the encodement technicians to remove all artificial encodements holding in the guilt you accepted from others.

Now I want you to create a different experience with this food. Experience this favorite food of yours in all its sensual luxury. Smell it and get excited about it. Imagine tasting it. Can you imagine it being different because you have removed from it the beliefs that result in guilt about having it?

Were you aware that what you were doing was accepting the beliefs of others about what is good and what is bad? But, you might say, "They are the authorities." Have you noticed that the more verbiage there is against eating disorders, the more eating disorders there are? There are many who have decided they have a particular eating disorder because they have read about it. They've accepted the beliefs of others about their body, what it should look like, and how it should respond. It is actually impossible from the way you have created yourselves to gain one pound from eating a slice of cake that has 500 calories in it. Aren't there about 3500 calories to a pound? Yet some people will eat one slice of cake and gain one or two pounds. Do you think that has anything to do with the cake? Absolutely nothing.

Q: When I think about my life when I was in my twenties versus now that I'm in my fifties, then, in general, food was something to eat as quickly as possible because I had a lot going on and I was excited to get on to the next thing. What I seem to see now in some people around me, and in myself, is that food is more of the point in life. I'm wondering if part of what is going on in our society is that we have people who are using food to make them feel better rather than enjoying their lives. Maybe that's a symptom rather than something that's scientific. That is my first question/comment.

The second is, we do have a physical body and there are certain things that enhance our body and chemical reactions that tend to imbalance our body—and everyone's body is different. Are you saying we can ignore that and do what we want all the time because we like it, like I could handle twenty-five pieces of cake every day and still be healthy?

A: The answer to that is yes and no. Are you aware of some people like Yogananda who have changed their body overnight? There are those who have the ability to do that. In some cultures, if you are slender that means you are impoverished. So they need more weight to display prosperity. Some can make those changes overnight and become fifty pounds heavier. There are also those whose bodies are healthy and they haven't had food or drink in twenty years. Yes, you can create that. You can do exactly what you want to do. However, you have to be disconnected from all beliefs others have told you and have very different beliefs about that cake. Can you do that?

Q: So, I could just live on cake if I wanted to and my belief systems supported that?

A: Correct. You could even live without food. That is the creative part within you. But, it is very difficult to do because you have to disconnect yourself from every belief that says you can't do that.

Q: Like my mother saying that I can only have one piece of cake.

A: Yes, that's right. And you can't have it unless you eat all of the food on your plate and especially if you don't eat those vegetables, right? You have all bought into the belief that you have to have certain things in order for the body to subsist. Yet I can tell you there are people on this planet who do not have that belief system—who could just eat cake and have all the nutrients their bodies need.

You've heard of the placebo effect, have you not? That is what happens when you believe that something will heal you and it's just a sugar pill. In your Western medicine, the placebo effect is almost always used as a negative. They would say it was just a placebo effect even though the person healed and was well.

I will tell you of a documented case of a man who had terminal cancer. He was convinced that if he received a certain experimental treatment, the cancer would be eliminated and he would be well. He begged and he begged to get on this trial but he did not fit the criteria for this research study. His physician did something very unethical. He gave the man an injection of something that really was nothing more than water and electrolytes, and told him he was part of the study. Remember that his body was literally getting ready to die. Once he had what he thought was this magic drug in his body, he recovered quickly and went home in two days, much to the surprise of everybody. He had been bedridden but he walked out.

He was fine for months. The doctor was puzzled, to say the least. Months later, the news reported this new form of chemo was ineffective. The man read that news and was in the hospital at death's door within hours. The doctor, thinking about all this, did something else unethical. He came in and told the man that he realized he had read the report about the chemo being ineffective. He said there is a newer, stronger version, and he told him that it is doing the trick. He gave the man what he had given him before, water and electrolytes, on the pretense that it was this better chemo. The man got stronger and went home the next day. Sometime after that, there was a report that the chemo was definitely proven to be ineffective. The man died in two days.

His beliefs, and it was nothing but his beliefs, kept him alive for some time. It truly is the tremendous power of the mind which changes the body. That man, by virtue of his mind and his beliefs, healed himself of cancer—twice. Yet, he was totally dependent upon the beliefs of others about the effect of the drug upon him. He healed himself of the cancer because he believed fully in the power of that substance outside of him because the authorities had said it would work. When it was proven that the drug did not work, he believed it even though his body had been doing well. This is a true story.

If you were totally disconnected from the belief that you had to have certain vitamins and minerals, and you had to have a certain balance in foods, and you had the belief you could eat all the cake, or whatever you chose, and you would be as healthy as you could be, then, yes, you could eat as many pieces of cake as you wanted and your body would be healthy. I'm using cake as an example because it is a dessert most people enjoy.

You must first disconnect yourself from the belief that you need various nutrients to be healthy. You can begin this process by working with your encodements. You can ask that all artificial and natural encodements holding in the words of your mother now be released. There will be consequences to this request. It can have a domino effect on all the beliefs you received from your mother— and what your mother's mother said and your mother's mother's mother. And we should get dad in there, too. Mothers usually have more to say about your eating but fathers become involved, also. You would need to disconnect yourself from all of this energy.

When you believed in what your mother said, you gave your power to your mother. That is how this life was devised. What better way to convince yourself you are not infinite and you are powerless than to have someone tell you how you have to eat and dress? Every human being has acquired tremendous adherence to beliefs. "All" you have to do is to disconnect yourself from those beliefs.

Be aware, there are many more beliefs you would need to disassociate yourself from for these new beliefs about eating and nutrition to take root. There are layers of beliefs. This is no easy task, but, if you made it your goal, you could do it.

Q: Regarding beliefs, there is faith and faith healing. I did ten days with a faith healer in Florida who has been known to help people heal their teeth—tooth decay, regenerate teeth, convert mercury amalgam fillings to gold and that sort of thing. Some people call him the tooth fairy. He's a reformed Baptist preacher so his style is still that way but he is truly compassionate. He's very Bible-based. I learned in those ten days that I don't have that kind of faith. He said that if you had the faith then the laying on of his hands would heal and many people experienced their teeth being healed. One thing I've learned about myself is that I have to feel something in order to believe something is changing. I wanted to regenerate worn down tooth enamel and grow my teeth back because my bite was all messed up. I've gradually been healing all of that. It's very interesting about beliefs because there are very few beliefs out there in the culture or even with holistic healing people that say you can grow your teeth back. I'm trying to find the triggers that will help me to go in that direction.

A: The first thing to do is to dismantle the belief that you have to feel something in order for it to happen.

Q: But, I enjoy feeling things. I believe I'm in a body for a reason. One of those reasons is to feel sensations and to experience through the senses.

A: Yes, you can have that enjoyment, but to make it a priority for something to happen in your life would be limiting. To have the sensation of slipping into a wonderful bath with fragrant oils, soft candle light and enjoyable music would be the kind of sensation you would want to enhance.

Q: In this case, I'm thinking of the sensation of vibration on a cellular level of the gums healing. Actually, I want to feel movement and life force energy in the teeth. I like feeling the energy move and the cells vibrate and making those electrical connections.

A: And you can enjoy that. But what if that is not how your teeth are going to regenerate—they are going to regenerate without the feeling?

Q: I'll take it, of course. But I'm not sure what I can do to align myself with that.

A: You do know what to do to align yourself with that. It is simply to recognize the fact that you have that belief and that it is mutable. It is not, shall we say, set in teeth (rather than in stone). It can change. The belief you have to feel things in order for them to be true can change. That is no different than your scientific community saying they have to see it in order for it to be true. So, the work you do with the Akashic Records, if you had to do it from a scientific basis, you wouldn't be able to do what you are doing, would you? You can see that your beliefs are at odds in different places, correct?

All of the beliefs pertaining to the development of your body are not only personal beliefs but also beliefs of the entire community. As we have said, this is something called the morphogenic field or matrix. You can choose to be different. That is what Jesus did. That is what Yogananda did. That is what Sai Baba does when he materializes things. That is what the saints of the Bible, or in India, Tibet or other places did and do.

The man you are speaking of is an alchemist. You can all be your own alchemist. He decided that was how he wanted to experience this lifetime—to awaken in some measure to the infinity of who he is. But he still had beliefs that it had to be Judeo-Christian based. Remember that Jesus was not a Christian.

Q: I experienced a spontaneous healing when I first connected deeply with the Akashic Records. It scared me so much that I kind of ran the other way. I'm wondering if I'm still holding onto that. It was so shocking to be physically healed in an instant. It was so shocking that I was crazy.

A: You have this energy within you that said, "Wait a minute. I'm not supposed to remember that I'm infinite and powerful." And so, you chose to run away from your power instead of embracing your power.

How many times have any of you had a hint of your power and you've run screaming in the other direction? By your choice, it is a game to keep you from recognizing you are infinite. All of you, when you shed your bodies, will discover the truth. Even now, in some way, you have said that you would like to discover the truth of who you are as an infinite being. It does not matter, and it is just as much fun, to play this life either way—what some call "awake" and some call "not awake." There is no difference in the quality of experience people have in their human game. When they leave this planet, they all discover the truth.

If you want to get in touch with the absolute power that you are, the creative energy that you have, you will come face-to-face with your belief systems that say you do not have that power. How do you recognize those belief systems? It is not in an intellectual matter. It is in a feeling manner. Fear, anger, sadness—they all can be used to keep you from recognizing your power. The incident described when tapping into the Akashic Records was fear. The fear showed her where she hid her power. She ran from her fear.

She could have instead turned to her fear and called in the encodement technicians, telling them, "I want to recognize, be aware of, and be involved in the power that I am, the love that I am, the infinite being that I am. I wish to experience this." You can ask them to assist you in releasing any encodements that are holding in that fear. You can tell them, "I want all of that energy, all of that thought, all of that creative power that went into this absolutely perfect creation I've made to hide my power. I'd like it back. Please remove all artificial encodements keeping me from my power. Please remove any natural encodements I was born with to keep me away from my power. Please remove those."

That sounds simple enough, doesn't it? Aaah, think about it. It unleashes a domino effect, a Pandora's box, where fears come up to be released. Remember, however, that in Pandora's box there was one thing left when everything else was out. The myth says it was hope. Let me re-write the myth and say it was love/power/ energy/Who You Are/the Love That You Are.

If you choose to go into this way of accessing your power and remembering who you are, you will have opportunities every day—sometimes every minute—to recognize that your power is hidden in that fear, in that anger, in that sadness, in that resistance. The encodement process will assist you. Ask your encodement technicians for all the energy and power you used to create this life of limitation to come back to you so you may create anew. It will happen slowly because that's usually how it is. Why? So you can savor it…just like you wanted to savor the feel of the energy.

Somebody could decide to have it happen instantly. You are an infinite being and you could make that decision on a soul level. Just because that's not usually how you have set up this life doesn't mean it couldn't happen. Nearly all of you, with few exceptions, have set it up to unfold gradually so you will experience the transformation.

There are those of you who have different jobs on the other side of the veil. Some of you may be aware of this. Some of you are teachers and instructors over there as well as here. Know this. Also, know that what you do on the other side of the veil may not have anything in particular to do with this incarnation. If you try to discover everything that you are doing on the other side, it will keep you from exploring who you truly are from the perspective of this side of the veil. Having said that, know that it doesn't matter what you do. It is all an amazing creation of the greatest illusion.

One of the major mental activities keeping everyone from their power is a word called *judgment*. When you judge something to be good or bad, to be evolved or not evolved, you are judging your own creation. You get to choose for yourself how you wish to experience your creation. Others will choose for themselves. It will have an impact on you because that is why you created that person, that situation. There are those in this country, the U.S.A., who are only vaguely aware of battles in other parts of the world. You may wonder how that could be true. They decided not to make that a part of their lives. They don't read newspapers or watch TV. Others make a judgment about their behavior.

There are people content with not being what you might call spiritual. Yet the reality is there is no one who is not spiritual. You cannot not be spiritual because you are spirit. It is just that there are those who have chosen not to be aware of their spiritual nature. You have a choice in how you experience yourself. At the same time, your choice does not change who you truly are.

Q: My question is: What energy is boredom? I'm not suggesting that I want to leave the planet. I love this place and it's really been a lot of fun. But it isn't fun anymore. What is this boredom?

A: Boredom is simply a hiding of your power. Boredom disguises your joy. As an infinite being, as Love Incarnate, you are Joy. You do not become joyful—you *are* Joy. What I would suggest is to begin to discover what belief systems are behind your boredom. Before you do that intellectual exercise, you could ask about artificial and natural encodements that have anything to do with boredom. Look at your life in all its areas. See in which area or areas you are not in acceptance of, but in denial or suppression of your feelings.

Q: My belief system is fun?

A: Exactly. In your belief system, is it permissible to have fun?

Q: Something has to happen out here for me to even interpret it as fun.

A: That's correct. If you grew up with the idea that you had to work hard with no joy and no fun, and fun ended when you were twelve or ten or three, then you have some deeply held beliefs. It could be you are now trying to break out of this. Look at the areas of your life in which you're not happy but are hiding it. You want to deny that you're unhappy because then you would have to do something about it, and you're afraid of what you would have to do.

Cathy Chapman

Of course, you can ask for help. Just be aware of possible consequences. You can use the encodement technicians on something as vague as, "Are there any artificial encodements holding in place the veil of my seeing the truth of - - - - - ?" And just list all the areas of your life: "...seeing the truth of my job; seeing the truth of my play time; seeing the truth of where I live and whom I live with. Am I enjoying having fun? Am I pleased and happy? Does what I do bring me joy?"

I've talked about joy. Do what brings you joy. Be in relationships that bring you joy. When you do the best thing for yourself, you are doing the best thing for everyone else because everyone else and how they respond to you is your creation. Three days from now, when you think of what you've read here, you may be absolutely astounded to remember that I said you have created me to say these words to you or you would not be reading them. Yes, I am your creation. Everyone who says anything to you is your creation. Not just your mirror—your creation. The words are as uplifting or painful as they are because, for some reason, you wanted to experience that in some way. They could be a reflection of you for you. They could be moving you in a different direction. Earlier I talked about choosing to leave a church, a family or a group. You created something in that experience to move you to a different place. Enjoy your creations; thank your creations; appreciate your creations.

Q: My understanding from what you're saying is that before we incarnated on the planet, we created our life from beginning to end. What about the concept of freedom of choice? Is there no randomness or freedom of choice in things that come up so we can choose how we react? Is it all created from the beginning?

A: That's a good question. It's all about your Soul Self. Why is it so important to be in touch with your Soul Self? Your Soul Self is driving the bus. Remember that you are the persona for the experience of your Soul Self. It is your Soul Self who makes choices. It sounds like you are just a puppet but that is not the case. That is a belief hiding power. As you come to be aware of your Soul Self and connect with your Soul Self more deeply, you will realize that you and your Soul Self are the same. You are an extension of it no matter what you call it, Soul Self or Higher Self. I will talk about how encodements will be changed by the decision of your Soul Self even though you are not consciously making the choices.

Yes, there can be randomness and, at the same time, there is not. This is a very complex process to understand. It doesn't make any difference whether you understand it or not. Any attempt to continue mentally working it out simply hides you from your power. You will not fully understand this process until you leave your body and return "Home." It is not the same thing as predestination, which you may have heard of from a religious perspective. But yes, everybody is predestined to go to heaven, if you want to use that term. In other words, everybody is going to finish this life and ultimately go "Home."

With the words you have said in a prayer Jesus taught you, "Thy will be done," think of it more as your Soul Self being the director of your play. Your Soul Self is the one who has full access to all of the information, limitlessly and infinitely.

Q: I want to ask about fear. It came up awhile ago. Fear has been a huge issue in my life and I still have a lot of fear. So, fear exists outside of our incarnation as a human being on the Earth?

A: It is a wonderful creation to keep you from realizing how infinite and powerful you are. You came here in the persona that you have, to let things unfold. You wanted to keep yourself from knowing who you truly are because if you knew, it wouldn't be any fun. Why wouldn't it be fun to suddenly realize that you are infinite? The game would be over.

Q: Why couldn't you realize you're infinite and still have fun being incarnate? Didn't Jesus?

A: Did he? He accepted his limitations in this physical realm, did he not? And yes, he did have fun but he wasn't totally in his infinity.

Q: Does fear exist in heaven?
A: Oh, heavens, no.

Q: Good, because one of my fears is that I'll take it with me when I go.
A: What I have done here is to challenge some of your belief systems. I've also purposely put your Soul Self in the place of God. Everything you believe about God, I'm saying can be true of your Soul Self. That can be a tremendous earthquake for some beliefs. Yes, you are an aspect of God. And, as this aspect of God, you created yourself to have a certain experience in the human game. Think of games where you have characters and you make choices about what they do. Your relationship between your persona and your Soul Self is similar, but not exactly. Your Soul Self has unlimited information and that information is filtered to you as you are unfolding your life—the game of your life. Just sit with this information and know that whether you accept my words or not, it doesn't matter. You, and everyone hearing or reading this, will hear or see their own words and what it is they need to help them unfold their lives in any way they so choose.

Your Soul Self may say, "Stage right," or "Stage left"; "Let's experience confusion now and allow the result to unfold." "Let's experience boredom and how I've created myself to be bored and how I'm going to handle that."

Q: That makes me think more about the question of having free will—that we have the free will to accept that experience and see what it's like, or we lose our conscious awareness and come into our ego self and make a decision not to. I think that's where free will comes in. We have the power to do that, but most of us on the planet walk around in our ego self rather than in our Soul Self. In the ego self, we're not too inclined to accept these uncomfortable things we've scheduled for ourselves. I know for myself that I'm aware that I've created this and know what's going on and can experience it and call back my power, yet I find that my free will from my ego self gets in there a lot and shuts it down. I just wanted to comment on that because I feel you are exactly right with what you are talking about. But we're really not there yet. It's our goal.

Concerning the comment about becoming our infinite self in an instant, my belief system says that it's not possible for me because that's not why I agreed to come. If I changed my belief about why I came, then I could do that. But I have a belief that says I needed to experience these things over this lifetime so that I would begin slowly to grow and understand who I really am. So I would get that deep within my heart, deep in my being, so it's integrated within me and I truly know it. It's not a mental knowing. I've spent many years in my mental and it's very different when you really get it and know who you really are. For me to give that up would be to go back to the infinite and not have the fullness of the experiences I agreed to have during the opportunity of this incarnation.

A: Yes, you've stated it very well. When you leave here having had those experiences, you look at everything you've done and you're truly excited about how you did it. You may even decide to try certain things again. "I barely touched on this experience here. I want to go again and really explore that." And, maybe you choose the experience on another planet with different beings or different souls.

There are those on this planet who love to delve into one thing, learning it and discovering how little they know of it the deeper they go into it. There is always more to learn. Then there are those who experience learning it and are then ready for a new experience. It doesn't matter which way you choose. There are those who say, "I've done this long enough; I'm bored. I want to try something different." That is what it would be like if you suddenly became infinite and there was no challenge in playing this human game anymore. Think of how excited you are when something comes to fruition or works out. I want you to know that you are even more excited about the bumps in the road that got you there. The satisfaction of accomplishing something yourself is tremendous.

Q: What you've just said applies to a new CD I've made. I could have said it was too hard to do, that I'm not capable of manifesting things that I start. Or I could have gone the other way and said that I'm going to ignore the prevailing consciousness that says this can't be done if you're not with a major company, I don't know how to do this, there's no way I can do it because I don't have the knowledge—and do it anyway. That's my freedom of choice. Either way I get to play this infinite game. It's like you always play the game you set up but you're free to take different pathways within that game. And it's all unfolding so I realize who I really am. Is that right?

A: That is right.

Q: So, whether I "fail" or "succeed" at any endeavor I try, it doesn't matter because it all serves for me to unfold eventually as a human being.

A: Yes, that is correct. Think about the satisfaction you had when you finally had the CD package ready to market. Then think about what it would have been like if, in the beginning, you had used your power to suddenly manifest it. Would it have been as much fun? *(No.)* That is why you have the struggle, the unfolding. You wanted to experience what that was like. You wanted to experience it in that way because it is more fun from the human standpoint to strive and to work at something.

Another point of information—your Soul Self has much to do with the part of the brain called the pre-frontal cortex in union with the heart. You can especially enter that area through your Heart Source.

I have given you many ways of looking at power and experiencing your power. The power you choose to hold is in your beliefs, in your encodement system. That will determine what you see, what you hear, what you smell. There are people who will read this and never understand much at all. Some will be distracted by noises from outside. Some will have faded off as they were reading.

That is an example of how you all end up with different information from the same stimulus.

Your beliefs determine everything that is going on in your energy. There are encodements for those beliefs. We have talked about this. You were born with cultural encodements for the cultures you planned to experience. If, for some reason, you choose to be in a different culture, it would assist you greatly to ask for encodements for that new culture to be created for you. You simply ask for an encodement shift, a culture shift.

If you want to fast-forward your ability to come into the knowledge and awareness of your infinite Self, discover where that information is hidden from you. You will find it in your fear, your anger, your relationships with other people, in your anxiety, in your boredom. It will be hidden there. Work with your encodement technicians to bring it out of hiding.

Be in communication with your Soul Self. And, know that *it does not matter* what choice you make. Yes, it will change the way the game plays out for you but, in the higher realms, it does not matter what choice you make. Everybody else will continue playing his or her game.

So, Dear Ones, that's enough for now. My blessings to each of you. I do place my hands upon you. Remember that I am multi-handed, and I now have one on the front and one on the back of your heart center and one on your head. This love is here for you. It is who you are, as we are all connected. I am Amma. I am the Divine Mother of the divine mothers. I am your mother. And you did grow in my womb.

Appendices

Who is God?

Now I would like to take this opportunity to answer a question asked of me. The answer will be in the context of power.

Question: Who is God according to your angle of vision? What is our goal when becoming self-realized? What is your view of devotion to God as the highest conception and goal of souls? What is your view of DEVOTION as the highest conception?

Amma: "God" has no definition. Those names you use for God, those names you have heard others use for God, are not the ultimate God. I have said that I am Amma, the Divine Mother of the divine mothers. I am the feminine aspect of God. Am I the "final, the highest" aspect of God? No, my Dear One, I am not. I also continue to grow and to expand. I continue to evolve into Who I Am.

When you ask for the "Who" of God, you are asking for a limit that is held within a name. There is no limit to God. God is creative force. God is Love Itself. God has no boundaries and has no definition. All the names of God that you have heard and will hear are simply monikers to attempt to make God fathomable to you. As unfathomable as you think God is, God is even more so.

Becoming self-realized is nothing other than coming to know who you truly are. You are infinite. You are divine. You are, yourself, creative force. I am not speaking of the persona who you think you are. I'm speaking of the infinite creative power you are who has developed this persona you believe is yourself to enjoy the world you live in. You may think you do not enjoy this world. That lack you feel is nothing more than your experience of limitation.

When you become what is called self-realized, you will realize your very self that nothing you see, hear, touch, or experience is important. Those who are self-realized know this. They do not tell many this because very few can understand this concept. As you do what leads you to the peace deep within you, you will grow closer to self-realization. The ones who are self-realized, and there are very few, have come into their full power. They re-member their power. They use it with joy and delight.

The greatest devotion is one of appreciation. Some traditions call it praise. Some, thankfulness. When you can truly appreciate every aspect of your life, every aspect of your creation, you have come to self-realization. You have come to true devotion. You have come into your power.

Amma's Information

Amma's introductory information is found in the book *Change Your Encodements, Your DNA, Your Life*.

When you are ready to expand your consciousness by tapping into the power hidden within your energy field, sign-up for Amma's daily e-mail course. A lesson will come each day to your in-box for a year. For her, the number of lessons corresponds to the number of days in a leap year. After all, you are "leaping beyond" the everyday human consciousness closer to that of your infinite self. Sign-up at www.AmmaTheDivineMother.com.

Look for the daily e-course in book form, *Heart Source: Break Through to Personal Power*, soon to be released.

Since not everyone feels motivated to participate in the daily course, there will be several small books excerpted from *Heart Source: Break Through to Personal Power*. The first of these, *Heart Source: Releasing Victim Consciousness* will be out soon. Others to follow include the topics of abundance, breaking curses, balancing genetic issues, and changing beliefs.

If you are ready to do your own self-healing and work to transmute darkness to light, become a member of the Spiritual LoveFare Team. You may find more information and register for the team at www.SpiritualLoveFare.com.

If you feel the motivation for a private session with Amma, please contact Cathy at Cathy@AmmaTheDivineMother.com. Amma enjoys assisting people in working with their encodements.

If you wish to be updated about Amma's activities, sign up for either the email course or the Spiritual LoveFare list. Cathy holds teleconferences with Amma about once a month. These are Amma's gift to you. She also holds longer teleconferences in which she asks for an offering of appreciation for that particular teleconference.

Additional Healing Opportunities

Cathy Chapman, PhD, is a mind-body psychotherapist and a powerful healer. She can assist you in moving beyond non-supportive beliefs and patterns. Learn more about her healing work and offer appreciation for the various healing tools available through her web site www.OdysseyToWholeness.com. For a powerful opportunity to participate in your own healing with a 60 second daily time commitment, go to www.GroupDistanceHealing.com.

Cathy also does telephone consults and distance healing. You may arrange for those by email at Cathy@OdysseyToWholeness.com. Although she does have a telephone number, your best chance to connect with her is through email.

Tools of Others

Shaina Noll and Cathy collaborated on a CD *A Place for You Here: A Loving Recreation of Your Birth Journey*. This is a powerful healing experience of your life from conception to birth. Shaina wrote a song of deep acceptance and healing for this CD. *A Place for You Here* is also the name of the song. You may obtain your own copy to use many times at www.ShainaNoll.com. While you're there, contact Shaina for one of her *Life Path Profiles*. Shaina is a gifted singer and intuitive.

Are you ready for information specifically for these amazing times? Go to *The New Era Times* at www.tnetimes.com. You'll find various columns and articles of interest for these amazing times. Cathy is often a guest columnist.

———•———

www.AmmaTheDivineMother.com
www.SpiritualLoveFare.com
www.OdysseyToWholeness.com

www.ingramcontent.com/pod-product-compliance
Lightning Source LLC
Chambersburg PA
CBHW060022100426
42740CB00010B/1565